Group's comforting children
in crisis

D1470517

Group

Loveland, Colorado
group.com

Group resources actually work!

This Group resource incorporates our R.E.A.L. approach to ministry. It reinforces a growing friendship with Jesus, encourages long-term learning, and results in life transformation, because it's

Relational
Learner-to-learner interaction enhances learning and builds Christian friendships.

Experiential
What learners experience through discussion and action sticks with them up to 9 times longer than what they simply hear or read.

Applicable
The aim of Christian education is to equip learners to be both hearers and doers of God's Word.

Learner-based
Learners understand and retain more when the learning process takes into consideration how they learn best.

Comforting Children in Crisis

Copyright © 2009 Group Publishing, Inc.

Visit our website: **group.com**

Credits
Contributors: Sharon Carey; Lisa Downs, LPC; Heather Dunn; Kevin Groeneveld, MS; Jan Kershner; Janna Kinner, MSW; Becki Manni; Larry Shallenberger; Shauna Skillern, LMFT; Linda Swindell, Ph.D.; Ron Welch, Psy.D.; Jennifer White, LCSW, CACII
Chief Creative Officer: Joani Schultz
Senior Developer: Patty Smith
Senior Project Manager: Pam Clifford
Copy Editor: Dena Twinem
Art Director: Andrea Filer
Book Designer/Print Production Artist: Pamela Poll Graphic Design
Cover Designer: Andrea Filer
Cover Photography: Copyright Veer
Illustrator: Pamela Poll
Production Manager: DeAnne Lear

Unless otherwise ~~noted~~ ...... quotations are taken from the *Holy Bible*, New Living Translation, copyright © 199~~6~~ ...... ~~permission of Tyndale House Publishers, In~~c., Carol Stream, IL 60188. All rights reserved.

Library of Congress ~~Cataloging-in-Publication Data~~

Comforting children in crisis.
    p. cm.
  ISBN 978-0-7644-3829-5 (pbk. : alk. paper)
  1. Consolation. 2. Suffering–Religious aspects–Christianity. 3. Child rearing–Religious aspects–Christianity. 4. Parenting–Religious aspects–Christianity. 5. Psychic trauma–Religious aspects–Christianity. 6. Loss (Psychology) in children–Religious aspects–Christianity. 7. Crisis management–Religious aspects–Christianity. 8. Christian children–Religious life. I. Group Publishing.
  BV4909.C67 2009
  259'.22–dc22

                                2008033812

10 9 8 7 6 5 4 3 2   17 16 15 14 13 12 11 10 09

Printed in the United States of America.

Contents

Introduction

It's not easy losing a parent. Or dealing with life's many changes. Or going through a tragic loss.

It's difficult for adults.

But it's amplified for children.

"Let the children come to me" (Mark 10:14b). This can be hard when tragedy and trials damage children. You want to help them grow closer to Jesus through difficult situations, but you don't know how.

Although it isn't easy going through trials, it's also tough being on the outside and trying to help children who are suffering.

You don't know what to do. You're worried about their feelings or stepping on their parents' toes or saying the exact *wrong* thing.

Of course you care—you love them! It isn't that you don't want to help—it's just that you don't know how.

Comforting Children in Crisis will help you come alongside children and families who are facing tough times. From care and counseling tips, to practical ideas for children's ministry, school, daycare, or home, to what to say and what not to say, this book offers insight after insight into how to care for hurting children.

Of course, it'd be great if you never had to pick up this book! But the reality is that everyone faces tough times—especially children and families. And they need your help.

So when someone you love is going through the pain of parents divorcing, dealing with bullies, or walking through major life changes… it's time to pick up this guide. Use the Table of Contents to find the specific hurt you're concerned about, and then flip to that section.

Once there, you'll find a **real-life narrative**—a story from someone who's been there. Sometimes they're inspiring, and you'll read how the support and love of a teacher, children's minister, daycare worker or another adult sustained a child through a hard time. Other times they're disappointing and tell stories of children left alone during tragedy or rejected during trial.

Either way, these stories will show you the importance of devoted adults.

Each section also includes **care and counseling tips** that will give you practical ideas for reaching out in love. From listening to children and families, to mediating in hurtful situations, to intentional reminiscing, these ideas will help you effectively support hurting children.

Next, you'll find **additional care tips** for your whole family, children's ministry or class. These practical ideas will help everyone support the hurting child or family during trials.

And finally, you'll find an invaluable section on **what to say and what not to say** to children touched by these situations. Children are very impressionable, and the words we use can help or hurt a child more than we know. This section will help you avoid the hurtful comments and use the helpful ones.

You'll also find useful boxes in each section that offer Scripture help, guidelines for referring your child or family to a professional counselor, and additional resources, such as books and websites, that you can use as you support your hurting child.

Our prayer for this book is that it will help you help a child during a difficult time. And in so doing, you'll help that child grow closer to Jesus because of the love you show.

The names and identifying information of the children and families who have shared their stories have been changed.

The information in this book is meant to be a guide for you to handle emergencies that children and families face. This is not professional advice meant to replace that which you would receive from licensed counselors or psychologists.

CHAPTER ONE

Abuse

Supporting Children Who Are Suffering

with counseling insights from **LISA DOWNS, LPC**

+ care tips from **LARRY SHALLENBERGER**

The Smith family, by all outward appearances, was the all-American, "all-church" family. Bob and Andrea were both working, professional parents, longtime church members, and deeply involved in church life. Andrea was an eight-year-member of the children's ministry team. Bob served as an elder. Their three children, Sally, Justine, and Kyle, attended every program the children's ministry had to offer. The view from the pew was that the Smiths had it all together.

Yet Bob was living proof that it's impossible to profile a pedophile. Bob wasn't the stereotypical seedy-looking guy patrolling his rusty van through school zones. Bob was a handsome realtor, connected on several community boards. And yet Bob's computer was filled with child pornography.

Andrea discovered the child pornography quite by accident. When she confronted Bob, he responded with sharp denial and excuses.

"A malicious virus must have placed those pictures on my computer."

Andrea wanted to believe him, and tried for several months. However, she had gnawing suspicions. Their sex life had been dead for, well, years. When Bob did ask for sex, he made requests that repulsed Andrea. Bob frequently slept in each of the children's bedrooms, saying Andrea was a loud snorer. Even though Andrea wondered if Bob had abused the children, she didn't have the emotional strength to face that possibility. Andrea struggled with assertiveness—partly because she had survived deep hurts from her own family growing up. Believing that her husband was capable of betraying *his* family was a thought too terrible to think.

That is, until one night when Andrea decided to check Bob's computer. Again, the computer was filled with pornography. Andrea's heart sank. That week, Andrea found a quiet moment to talk to each of her children, and her worse fears were confirmed. Both Sally and Justine told her, in guarded sentences, that their father had touched them sexually. Kyle, the youngest, refused to talk and became angry when Andrea pressed him for information.

Crushed, Andrea confided in the senior pastor for support. The pastor wisely counseled Andrea to separate from Bob and to demand he leave the home. The pastor also insisted that Andrea call the police and report the child pornography on the computer and the abuse. At church, they told only the children's pastor of the situation. It wasn't necessary to share the information with the volunteer team.

The senior pastor helped Andrea refer the three children to professional counseling to help them feel safe and begin to talk about the abuse. As a result of Justine's disclosures during private counseling, criminal charges were filed against Bob.

Bob tried, on a few occasions, to make contact with his children at the church. It's possible that Bob's unauthorized attempts to contact the children were attempts to either bribe or intimidate his children into silence. The church was able to deny Bob access to his children because they already had strict pick-up and dismissal policies in place.

Bob tried to woo Andrea, perhaps in an attempt to get her to drop the charges. When that approach didn't work, Bob angrily blamed his wife for the abuse, claiming that it was her inadequacies in the bedroom that drove him to sexual deviancy. However, through the support of caring pastors and trusted friends at church, Andrea was able to resist Bob's varied approaches to control her.

During the months leading up to the trial, the church provided Andrea with the emotional scaffolding she needed to take care of herself and her children. Plus, the church became a safe, fun place for the children to temporarily escape the realities of their family and to learn about the love and comfort that Jesus offers.

When the day finally came for Justine to testify against her father, a few of the pastors and family friends came to the courthouse to provide emotional support to both Justine and Andrea. Even with this support, Justine was unable to provide compelling testimony against her father. The pressures were simply too much for a child to handle.

Bob did eventually serve prison time for possessing child pornography. And through the process of protecting her children, Andrea confronted her own childhood issues. She's been faithful in making sure her children get the help they need. Justine and Sally are both teenagers now, and both benefited from years of counseling to deal with their father's betrayal. Kyle is in the middle school ministry. He deals with academic problems and occasionally fights with other children. Kyle hasn't been as open as his sisters in counseling and will someday still need to confront the abuse that his counselors suspect happened.

While this story doesn't end with "and they lived happily ever after," the Smiths are grateful for the support and help they received at church. They learned that the church can be a place of healing and love, and perhaps one day they can use this trial to help another family in trouble.

Care and Counseling Tips

THE BASICS

Child abuse is shocking and all too common. Someone is abusive if he or she fails to nurture a child, physically injures a child, or relates sexually to a child. Physical abuse often garners the most attention in the news, but the more subtle forms of abuse, such as neglect and emotional abuse, can be just as detrimental. The first step in helping abused or neglected children is learning to recognize the signs of child abuse and neglect.

Be aware that these signs may not always point to child abuse.

TYPES OF CHILD ABUSE
+ Emotional

Emotional abuse is any attitude, behavior, or failure to act that interferes with a child's mental health or social development. It can range from a simple verbal insult to an extreme form of punishment. Emotional abuse is almost always present when other forms of abuse are present. Emotional abuse can have the deepest effect on the mental health of a child.

Signs: apathy (not caring), depression, choosing not to play or be involved in activities, hostility, aggression

+ Neglect

Neglect is a common type of child abuse. More children suffer from neglect than from physical and sexual abuse combined. Yet victims of neglect often go unnoticed because neglect is an act of omission. The child may be ignored, not fed, or have medical needs that are left untreated. A single incident of neglect might not be considered child abuse, but repeated neglect is definitely abuse.

Signs: lack of supervision, not being properly dressed for weather, wearing the same clothes repeatedly, hoarding food, complaints of constant hunger, frequent illness due to poor nutrition or lack of proper medical attention.

+ Physical

Physical abuse is defined as any injury to a child that is a result of physical aggression. This aggression may include slapping, beating, or hitting a child, as well as shaking, biting, or kicking. Children who survive physical abuse are left with severe emotional scars. And as we all know from news accounts, not all children survive physical abuse.

Signs: welts, bruises, or burns, often in unusual places on the body such as the child's back, eyes, mouth, or thighs

+ Sexual

Sexual abuse is any form of sexual act between an adult and a child. Adults who sexually abuse children may do so by fondling or touching private body parts. They may force a child to undress or force a child to watch them undress. Adults who sexually abuse may also force a child to watch others engage in sexual intercourse or introduce them to pornography.

Signs: withdrawing, refusing to engage socially, refusing to undress for sports or other activities, exaggerated interest in sex, acting out sexually with other children, becoming seductive toward others, fear of contact such as a pat on the arm or hug, masturbation, acting out sex with dolls or toys

SCRIPTURE HELP

+ Proverbs 31:8-9
+ 2 Samuel 22:2-4
+ Jeremiah 29:11-13
+ Psalm 23
+ Romans 8:15-16
+ Psalm 55
+ Ephesians 6:1-4
+ Psalm 61:3
+ 1 Peter 5:7
+ Psalm 82:3-4
+ Revelation 21:4

Care Tips

Abusers are often people the child knows and trusts—as a result, children may love those who are hurting them. This makes it difficult for children to reveal the abuse because they fear getting the abuser in trouble.

A child may talk to you about abuse because he or she trusts you and wants to share the burden. Hearing a child talk about abuse is difficult. Your reaction is important.

+ Remain calm.

Speak in a calm and gentle voice so the child feels safe. Encourage the child to use his or her own words, and don't find fault or question whether the child is being truthful. Children seldom lie about any type of abuse they are enduring. Ask simple yet direct questions. But don't try to investigate—leave interviewing to trained professionals who can speak with the child in a nonthreatening way.

+ Reassure the child.

If a child discloses abuse, it's imperative to say you believe the disclosure and you will do whatever you can to create a safe environment. It's important to say that the child is not guilty and is not responsible for the abuse. Assure the child that he or she did not do anything wrong, and praise the child for having the courage to come forward. However, don't make promises you can't keep, such as promising to keep the disclosure a secret. But do reassure the child that you will only disclose the conversation to those who can help the child.

+ Seek help.

There is help and support available to the child. When you have enough information to make an informed report, stop the discussion. See the Reporting Child Abuse box on page 20.

Counseling Tips

If a child has been a victim of any type of abuse, it's important that you provide protection, love, and support. A child who has been the victim of prolonged abuse usually develops low self-esteem, has feelings of worthlessness, and often develops a distorted view of relationships with others. If you suspect a child may be dealing with abuse, here are some ways you can begin to help.

+ Pay attention.
Children often give verbal or physical cues that provide possible evidence of abuse. They may express a wish not to be alone with certain adults. They may use sexual language or make subtle remarks to other kids about the abuse. They may mention sleep problems or talk frequently about nightmares.

+ Create a safe place.
Abused children have been pressured, lied to, tricked, and emotionally tossed around. Give the child your unconditional love and support. The child may or may not be comfortable with touch. Be careful when giving pats on the back or hugs. Take your cues from the child.

+ Respect the privacy of the child.
It's best not to involve too many people in the child's abuse disclosure. If you feel you need to let someone know, other than the authorities, ask the child (and parents if appropriate) first, and find out how he or she feels about it. Don't discuss the situation with others in front of the child or other children.

+ Gather information.
If a child wants to talk about the situation or abuse, listen supportively but don't pry. The purpose of your discussion is to gather enough information to make an informed report. It's not your job to prove that the abuse happened.

Choose your language and questions carefully as you try to assess the situation. For example, if you suspect abuse because you see a suspicious bruise or injury, you might say, "That looks like it hurts. Would you like to talk about how you got it?" Let the child respond in his or her own words. Avoid asking "why" questions such as, "Why did your dad hit you?" Abused children don't know or understand why they're being abused.

+ Be honest.

Be honest about what you can and can't do for the child. A child may ask you to promise not to tell anyone about the abuse, or a child may ask if he or she can come home with you. Explain that because you love the child, you'll have to tell someone who can help protect the child. Let the child know you believe him or her and that you don't blame the child for the situation.

WHEN TO REFER

+ If you suspect a child has been abused.

You should alert the authorities. See the Reporting Child Abuse box on page 20.

+ After abuse has been reported.

If children are able to talk about the abuse, have plenty of loving support at home or church, and are not displaying symptoms, it's possible they may have resolved the issue on their own. However, it's not a good idea to make that decision without consulting a professional who is well-versed in counseling abused children. A skilled counselor can encourage children to express their feelings through play, drawing, or writing letters. Counseling should start as soon as possible after the abuse is discovered. Families are most open to counseling while they are still in crisis mode because they are searching for support and answers.

Additional Care Tips

+ Acknowledge that abuse is a problem.

Acknowledge that child abuse, including sexual abuse, is a major concern for your ministry. Raise awareness of the reality of abuse and neglect by setting aside a Sunday to promote child protection and to celebrate children and the family. Look for educational materials and programs to aid your ministry in raising awareness about abuse.

+ Train ministry staff.

Train ministry leaders and volunteers to recognize the symptoms and signs of all forms of child abuse. Train them to work with victims and their families and to make immediate referrals for counseling services.

+ Support the family or child in need.

The family of an abused child will experience a variety of feelings and emotions and will need your support as they seek legal and professional advice. Parents often feel guilty for not having done enough to protect the child. Remind the family that you are praying for them, and offer to pray *with* them. Offer to attend professional and legal appointments with the family.

+ Educate parents.

Offer parenting classes or seminars to decrease the likelihood of abuse. Educate parents about the effect their own histories have on the way they parent their own children. Talk with parents about how to control anger. Suggest putting a child in timeout or giving themselves a timeout so everyone can calm down. Remind parents to count to 20 or to call a friend when they're feeling out of control. They can also call the 1-800-4-A-CHILD hot line.

+ Educate children.

Children need to know that the safety rules about safe touch apply all the time—not just with strangers—because kids are often sexually abused by people they know and trust. Abusers seldom need to use physical force to get a child to participate in sexual activities—they take advantage of the child's trust or friendship and use threats to keep the activity a secret. If a child is taught to firmly say "no," the abuser will realize that the child can't be easily manipulated.

Unfortunately, abusers are often able to use threats with success because kids are taught to believe and obey adults. Children need to know that their bodies belong to them and they have a right to decide how and when anyone touches them. Explain that if someone tries to touch them in ways that don't feel good, they have the right to say no. Remind children that if they're abused and they tell someone who doesn't believe them, they need to keep telling until someone finally does believe.

+ Provide information and resources.

Include information in your church bulletins and newsletters about child abuse and local resources to deal with it. Keep an updated list of resources for abused children and their families. Include books related to child abuse in your church library. Your local social services agency is a good place to start gathering resources.

+ Have a plan.

Have a plan of action if abuse is discovered or disclosed. Make sure that all members of your staff understand that the goal should be to refer the victim to professional help as soon as possible. The goal is not to investigate, not to prove allegations, and not to counsel (at least initially).

The goal is to get immediate professional help for the victim. Not doing so can cause long-lasting pain and can even taint an investigation. Bottom line? Seek professional assistance right away!

What Not to Say

+ "You shouldn't get angry at God."

Allow a child to express anger to God for not preventing the abuse. Scriptures are filled with laments of people who worked through disappointment with God.

+ "Did _____ ever happen to you?"

Never ask leading questions. Young children want to please adults and are susceptible to saying whatever they think you want to hear. Instead, just listen to the child, then say, "Thank you for telling me about this." Assessing the facts in a case of suspected abuse is a task reserved only for trained professionals.

+ "I can keep this secret."

Tell the child that your first responsibility is to protect children from danger. You can't keep secrets that lead to someone being hurt.

+ "You should have told me sooner."

It takes a great deal of courage for a child to disclose abuse. The child needs to be assured that he or she did the right thing by telling a trusted adult.

+ "I don't want to talk about this."

If you're uncomfortable talking with the child about the details of the abuse, find someone who is willing to do so. The child will sense if you're overwhelmed by the information, and this will only increase the child's feelings of shame and guilt.

+ "Why were you alone with this person?"

Remember that most children are abused by people they love or trust. An abused child needs reassurance that he or she didn't do anything to cause the abuse and it was the adult who was wrong. The child needs to know that you're open to hearing anything he or she has to share.

What to Say

✚ "I'm sorry this happened to you."

Empathizing with the child will demonstrate acceptance, support, and love for the child.

✚ "Together we'll get help so you can feel safe."

This will send the message that you're willing to protect the child from further abuse. Let the child know that you'll be taking steps to promptly stop the abuse. The child may fear retaliation for disclosing the abuse. It's important to inform the child that you'll be calling someone whose job it is to keep children safe. Assure the child that this is a safe person who will listen, ask questions, and help.

✚ "I believe you."

Abused children are often told by the abuser that no one will believe them if they tell. Abused children need to know that they are not to blame and that it was wrong for an adult to ask them to keep this type of secret.

✚ "It's not your fault."

Children have a naturally egocentric outlook—and thus, the natural tendency to think that they are somehow responsible for the abuse. You can reassure the child that he or she is not to blame.

✚ "You can take your hurt and anger to God."

You simply don't have the ability to explain why the abuse happened. But your words can give a child permission to process the resulting emotions with God.

+ "I'll do everything I can to keep you safe."

While you can't promise to keep the child from ever being hurt again, you can commit to being his or her advocate. You can promise to report the abuse to authorities.

ADDITIONAL RESOURCES

(out of print)

+ Books

The Color of Secrets: Encouraging Children to Talk About Abuse. Kimberly Steward. Park Forest, IL: Doghouse Press, 2003.

Kids Helping Kids: Break the Silence of Sexual Abuse. Linda Lee Foltz. Pittsburgh, PA: Lighthouse Point Press, 2003.

I Told My Secret: A Book for Kids Who Were Abused. Eliana Gil. Royal Oak, MI: Self-Esteem Shop, 1986.

When Your Child Has Been Molested: A Parent's Guide to Healing and Recovery. Kathryn B. Hagans, Joyce Case. San Francisco, CA: Jossey-Bass; Reprint edition, 1998.

+ Online Resources

www.darkness2light.org
www.childabuse.com
www.childwelfare.gov

REPORTING CHILD ABUSE

Your response to a report of child abuse is important. If a child discloses an incident of abuse, it's your primary job to listen, to record the information that he or she discloses, and then report to your state's department of public welfare. In the United States, Canada, and many other countries, if you're aware that a child has been abused, you are legally required to report the abuse to authorities. Some states provide a "clergy exemption," which allows a pastor the option to report abuse if the disclosure was acquired in the context of a confession or a counseling session. However, this exemption usually applies only to ordained clergy—consult your state's mandated reporting laws to see how they apply to you.

Anonymous reports are accepted in all states. Actual injury is not a prerequisite to making a report; abuse should be reported if a child is in danger of serious injury. Almost all states have a specific law that makes failure to report suspected abuse or neglect a crime.

If you are concerned about making the report, contact your local child protective agency for assistance. If you feel the child is in immediate danger, call your local law enforcement agency right away. Keep in mind that you don't need to know all the specifics to make a report.

Contact the local child protective services or local law enforcement to ask questions regarding reporting child abuse. These numbers are listed in your local phone book, or call 1-800-4-A-CHILD. Your courage in making the report may be what it takes for the family to get the support and resources it needs to be healthy and safe.

CHAPTER TWO

Bullying
Helping Children Deal With Tough Relationships

with counseling insights from **KEVIN GROENEVELD, MS**
+ care tips from **SHARON CAREY**

As I prepared for Sunday's lesson on David and Goliath, I considered ways my fourth-graders might be asked to be brave like David. I thought about scary visits to the dentist, standing in front of classmates, times of illness, unexpected moves, and new schools—all scenarios I thought would apply. One thing I didn't think of turned out to be the most powerful challenge of all for my kids.

At the close of the Bible story, Jamie said, "Goliath reminds me of Bobby Webster." Several other students nodded in agreement. And with those words began a telling discussion about the bullying "giants" who taunted and tormented the lives of many of my kids.

Jamie told of his ongoing battle with classmate Bobby Webster. Bobby was tall for his age and apparently used his size and strength to administer one-sided doses of intimidation to anyone he thought was weaker. Jamie was a mild-mannered boy—studious, quiet, and as small in stature as Bobby Webster was large. It was that obvious difference Bobby set out to exploit. Jamie was pushed aside at the drinking fountain, slammed in a game of Dodgeball, stared down in the hallway, shoved into a wall, had school supplies stolen, and received a regular dose of hurtful name-calling.

"I take the long way to the bus stop and make sure other kids are there so it's not just me and Bobby," explained Jamie. Meeting Bobby in an empty restroom or hallway struck fear in the heart of this young David.

As we talked, I realized that Jamie wasn't the only one who had fallen victim to a personal Goliath. It seemed that nearly every child in my class had suffered the sting of a bully's words or actions.

Samantha shared how three classmates had recently joined together in deliberately excluding her. "They say I'm fat because I can't run fast. They got mad at me because I made our team lose a race last week," she said. The girls refused to sit with her at lunch, ignored her in gym class, and deliberately excluded her from a slumber party. Samantha didn't buckle under their snubbing, though, and I was grateful to hear that her parents encouraged her to react with kindness, not revenge.

Max's reaction to bullying wasn't quite so admirable—at least at first. A sharp, energetic child, Max had struggled early on in school, often missing assignments and important information shared in class. In time, his parents discovered his moderate hearing loss. With the help of hearing aids, Max made definite improvements. However, adjusting to wearing hearing aids was easy compared to the teasing that followed. A classroom bully set his sights on making Max's life miserable. The bully would purposely speak softly or mumble, then laugh at Max for not being able to hear him. As time went on, the taunting grew into deliberate acts of aggression.

For a while, Max dealt with the ridicule by simply ignoring it, but as it grew worse, so did his reaction. Finally, he took a lesson from his bullying classmate and looked, in turn, for those he could intimidate. He started aimless fights with his siblings, teased younger children at the bus stop, and even treated his pets with an aggression that was not at all typical of his kind nature. In only a short time, Max was turning into a bully himself.

Max's parents quickly addressed the issue. Recognizing their son's actions as a compensation for his own feelings of insecurity, they approached him firmly but with compassion. By the time Max entered my class, he had learned considerable control and had grown in confidence.

As our classroom discussion time came to a close, I thanked the kids for sharing their stories so openly with one another. As we prepared to close in prayer, Max spoke up with a suggestion. "We should form a Sticks and Stones Club." He explained that whenever someone in his family is upset about receiving undeserved or cruel treatment from another person, they hold a meeting of the Sticks and Stones Club. They pass around a twig and a rock and pray together. The sticks pray for the family member to stand strong and stick up for what's right. The rocks pray for the enemy to become a friend.

I quickly reached for a pencil and wadded up a piece of paper, impromptu stick and stone. We followed Max's suggestion and prayed for one another that day. At home, on my desk, I keep a pebble and twig. I never teach a lesson on David and Goliath without recalling the prayers of the Sticks and Stones Club.

SCRIPTURE HELP

+ **1 Samuel 17**
+ **Psalm 32:7**
+ **Psalm 91:11**
+ **Proverbs 15:1**
+ **Luke 6:27-31**

+ **Luke 6:35**
+ **1 Corinthians 13:4**
+ **Ephesians 4:31-32**
+ **1 Peter 3:9**

ADDITIONAL RESOURCES

+ Online Resources

www.family.org (Focus on the Family)

www.pacerkidsagainstbullying.org (National Center for Bullying Prevention)

www.loveourchildrenusa.org

www.CBHMinistries.org and www.keysforkids.org

www.stopcyberbullying.com

Care and Counseling Tips

THE BASICS

Bullying is the deliberate attempt by a person or group to harm or intimidate others. One of the first steps to stopping bullying behaviors is to recognize the signs and symptoms. But be aware that bullying often happens right under the nose of a caring adult. Bullying can be subtle, so you need to know what to look for. It may come in three forms: physical, verbal, or social. The following signs and symptoms will help you identify when someone is being bullied.

+ Physical

While physical bullying is the most common form adults look for, it's often the least common form of intimidation in children. And even when physical bullying is present, the signs are often subtle and can be mistaken for various activity-related injuries. For example, you might notice bruises or abrasions that are difficult to explain. Further, if a child complains of feeling sick without showing symptoms of an illness, shows uncharacteristic nervousness, poor posture, or a low energy level, bullying may be the cause.

+ Verbal

Verbal bullying may take the form of jeers, taunts, put-downs, and insults—all devastating to a child's self-esteem. Keep in mind that bullies are masters at plying their trade out of the earshot of adults. If you suspect bullying is taking place among the children you minister to, you're probably correct.

Emotional reactions can range from increased fear and anger to withdrawal. Watch for unusual outbursts of anger, a significant decrease in spoken words, and a definite increase in crying and sadness.

+ Social

Social bullying can be more powerful than either physical or verbal bullying, and it's the form most favored by girl bullies. The bully shuns and ostracizes the victim from the group. Signs of social bullying may include spreading gossip and rumors, the deliberate exclusion or isolation of a child, and hostile body language or expressions. Rolled eyes, aggressive staring, and derogatory gestures often take place behind an adult's back.

Bullied children may refuse to attend school, avoid certain activities and children, cling to loved ones they trust, develop a pattern of playing alone, or have an unhealthy attachment to one or both parents.

WHEN TO REFER

Refer the family to a professional counselor in any of these situations:

+ The bully becomes violent or threatens violence.
Bullying can have criminal implications. If physical injury or personal threats of violence are associated with bullying, help the family contact the proper authorities. This might include school administration, social service agencies, or local law enforcement.

+ The victim becomes violent or threatens violence.
It's easy for a victim of bullying to "snap" and harm others when the bullying gets out of hand. Any threat of violence should prompt a referral to a professional counselor. Any actual violence should prompt a call to the authorities and a professional referral.

+ You notice signs of depression.
Depression is a serious concern in young people (see Chapter 5). If you notice signs or symptoms of depression as a result of bullying, seek professional help.

Care Tips

If you suspect that bullying behavior is occurring, here are some steps you can take.

+ Pay attention to targeted kids.
If you hear kids refer to another child as a "loner," there's a good chance that child is being targeted. Hone your listening skills. Be alert for telltale signs.

+ Teach children how to respond.
Don't let any situation reach the "boiling point." Encourage kids to talk to a trusted adult long before exploding in response to bullying.

+ Encourage kids to report bullying.
Teach your kids that it's not only OK, it's the right thing to do, when they report bullying to a trusted adult. Encourage kids to stand up for themselves and others—either during the incident or by reporting it. Make sure that both bystanders and targets know that reporting bullying is not tattling.

+ Deal with bullies sensitively.
Understand that bullying children may be bullied at home. Change the pattern by encouraging good behaviors and creating situations that'll help these kids succeed in "being good." Give bullies the opportunity to serve others and experience the positive emotions associated with putting someone else first.

Counseling Tips

Keep in mind that a child who is bullied may feel helpless, scared, hurt, angry, and even guilty. In your counseling with the bullied child and his or her family, you have a great opportunity to teach biblical principles of true strength. Remember: Counseling is a combination of teaching, coaching, and discipleship.

+ Allow physical movement.
Try to counsel children in a place where they can move around. Boys, especially, usually become more verbal when physical movement is allowed. Invite the family to sessions where you can talk about and practice self-defense techniques. Keep in mind the importance of teaching a child how to respond to, but not initiate, physical contact. (You may want to contact your local social services or law enforcement agencies to find experts on self-defense techniques.)

+ Work on emotional development.
Your tendency may be to focus on hurt and anger. Initially, this is a good approach. But some children believe that anger is a sin. It's not. Explain that it's how a child *reacts* to the anger he or she is feeling that's key. As you get to know the child's personality, you'll recognize emotions that need more of your counseling attention. Role-playing often helps a child practice displaying healthy emotions.

+ Practice what you preach.
Look at your behavior toward kids. If you find that there's a little bully lurking in you, work on eliminating the tendency. Then be consistent in how you deal with bullying behaviors. Teach that bullying is not going to be tolerated—end of story.

Additional Care Tips

While schools have come under scrutiny because of violent incidents, churches often feel exempt from having to deal with the bullying issue. Church is supposed to be a safe place, right? But the truth is that bullying happens wherever kids are. As a children's minister, you can take concrete, practical steps to thwart bullying and to build a caring community among the children you shepherd. Here's how:

+ Don't minimize or disregard instances of bullying.
Whether it's reported by a child or observed by an adult, take the report seriously. Don't indulge in looking the other way and thinking "Kids will be kids."

+ Put in place no-nonsense anti-bullying procedures.
Your classroom code should be that every child is valuable and unique, and no child will be left out or hurt. Create a zero-tolerance atmosphere that says "No bullying allowed!"

+ Don't resolve the situation yourself.
Doing so only reassures the bully that his or her target is weak.

+ Don't tell the target to avoid the bully.
This doesn't solve the problem—it's only a superficial, temporary fix.

+ Don't confront the bully or the bully's parents alone.
Bullying is often a learned behavior, and during a confrontation you may find yourself demeaned by the bully or the bully's family. Have backup at the meeting.

+ Make sure a member of your ministry team gives special attention to the target.

Spiritual effects of bullying can be difficult to see, but they have their root in doubt that God is a loving protector. Symptoms may include an unwillingness to pray or read the Bible; critical talk about God, self, or others; and unusual or strange questions about God's love for everyone. Be ready to meet these symptoms head-on, consistently reminding the child of God's unchanging nature, love, and provision. Be ready to offer examples from your own life of God's loving nature.

+ Emphasize that God loves each unique child.

Encourage every child to participate in a "Unique Talent Show" to strengthen children's self-esteem. Celebrate the fact that God has given each child unique gifts and abilities.

CYBERBULLYING

Cyberbullying is the use of electronic communication to torment others. With the increase in Internet use and other technology, bullies have additional avenues in which to carry out their cruelty. Here are a few tips to prevent or address cyberbullying:

• Encourage parents to have strict guidelines for the use of electronic communication devices, including locating computers in the safest, high-traffic places of the home.

• Warn children and their families of the danger associated with cyberbullies. Bring in special speakers to raise the level of awareness and to educate parents about cyberbullying.

• Encourage children to save threatening e-mails or text messages to show to their parents or teachers.

What Not to Say

Every bullying situation has unique circumstances. Try to consider the history, current facts, and future implications of each situation.

+ "You just need to toughen up."

Such comments are insensitive and will hurt the child and make him or her feel even weaker. It may be that the child is already acting as "tough" as he or she can. Teach kids to advocate for themselves by talking to a trusted adult before the situation escalates.

+ "God will always protect you from being hurt."

While God *does* protect us, sometimes he allows difficult things to happen. And we can learn and grow from these things. Pray with the child for strength.

+ "You need to learn to fight back."

Encouraging a child to use physical force such as kicking, hitting, or pushing to deal with a bully often makes matters worse by adding fuel to the fire. A child should learn how to stay safe and seek help from an adult rather than reacting in anger and violence.

+ "Sticks and stones can break your bones, but words can never hurt you."

Words *do* hurt. Often the cruel jeers and taunts of a peer are more painful than a broken bone and carry long-term impact.

What to Say

✚ "You did the right thing by telling me."

This validates a child's difficult decision to bring the matter to an adult's attention.

✚ "I care about you."

This is always a good thing to say in a difficult situation.

✚ "You're a cool kid, and God has great plans for your life."

Let children know that they are uniquely created, gifted, and valued by God. Help kids develop healthy self-esteem based on their worth to God and an awareness of his great love for them.

✚ "Let's pray for you and your enemy."

Prayer turns the focus away from the bully and onto the greatness of God—who is more powerful than even the biggest bully. Pray with the bullied child and together ask for God's help—share the weight of this difficult situation.

✚ "Even Jesus had to face bullies."

Jesus had his share of enemies. Remind your students that God's Son understands how it feels to be betrayed, rejected, and hurt by others. He stood strong and loved others even when they treated him badly. We can follow his example.

CHAPTER THREE

Changing Family Dynamics
Supporting Children
Through Family Changes

with counseling insights from RON WELCH, PSY.D.

+ care tips from BECKI MANNI

Kelly is a fifth-grade girl. She is dealing with the adoption of an older sibling in the past year and how this addition to the family has changed her world.

Comforting Children in Crisis: *When did you first know your parents would be adopting?*

Kelly: I've heard my parents talking about the possibility since school started. They sat down and talked to me about it when we were on Christmas break. They said it looked as if the adoption would go through. Abby was living in an abusive home situation and had been taken out of her parents' house. Her parents' rights were taken away, and that made it possible for her to be adopted. When my parents came to talk to me about it I felt so sorry for her and I wanted right away for her to come live with us.

CCC: *What was that process like?*

Kelly: At first she came to visit for a couple of afternoons with her social worker. Then after a while, she started coming to stay over for the weekends. Then there was a visit with just the social worker to see if our home was a good one. And then we also had to go to family counseling a couple of times. They asked us all kinds of questions about how we get along, if we have chores, where we go on vacation, and stuff like that. We all really liked Abby, and she seemed to fit into our family really well. I have three younger brothers, and I guess for all of us it was kind of like an adventure. We felt like we were rescuing the princess in a fairy tale.

CCC: *What was it like when Abby finally moved in?*

Kelly: It was really hard. She's a year older than me but she is so needy. I mean, she had to go everywhere with me, and all my friends didn't really want her there. She got mad over the littlest things, and then she would scream and call us names and slam her door. One time she even kicked a hole in my bedroom door because I wouldn't let her wear my favorite jean jacket. She cried all the time, and my parents had to spend more time with her than with me or my brothers. I used to be my daddy's little princess, but now I don't know if he even knows I'm around anymore.

Abby didn't do very well in school either. So my parents always had to go down to the middle school to talk to her teachers or pick her up from detention.

CCC: *How has this affected your family?*

Kelly: Well, it's not as much fun to be together as it used to be. We live in the mountains, and we like to do a lot of outdoors kind of stuff. At first we thought she liked to do that stuff, too. When she would come to visit, we would all teach her stuff like how to ski, how to swing on the rope swing out back, or how to do the chores with the rabbits and stuff. But now that she lives here, she's different. She gets cold real easy when we ski, and she wants to sit in the lodge all the time. Since we can't stay in the lodge alone, I have to stay with her because I'm the oldest and a girl. I miss all the good runs with my brothers. She's always worried about her hair and makeup, so she won't play outside with us. And when it comes to chores, she always seems to find another place she has to be so my brothers and I get stuck cleaning the cages and feeding the rabbits.

CCC: *How has your family changed?*

Kelly: I'm not sure, but sometimes it feels like she wants to make us mad or maybe to be as sad as she is. I hear her crying herself to sleep almost every night, and she has a lot of nightmares. I know she didn't have a good family, but I wonder sometimes if she wants to wreck this one, too. My mom says it will get better, but I don't know if I want to wait that long.

I mean, I want it to go back to the way it was. I know we should care about her and all, but sometimes I just want to send her back to Seattle.

CCC: *Have you talked to your parents about how you feel?*

Kelly: No, I just try to be a good girl so I don't cause any more problems for my parents. They are trying so hard, and I know they want to do something nice for Abby. I don't want to add to their problems, but sometimes I get really jealous when I see her getting all the attention, and then she doesn't even appreciate what we are doing for her. I know Jesus wants us to love everyone, but she makes it really hard to even like her.

CCC: *What do you think might help make the situation easier for you?*

Kelly: Sometimes I really need a vacation from that girl. And I could really use someone to talk to and explain that I don't hate her, I just don't know how to like her anymore. I wish I could talk to someone who has had to do this like me and ask how they did it. I would like to have my parents ask about how I am without always reminding me of how much I am supposed to love her. I want it to be OK to be mad sometimes.

CCC: *Anything else you would like people to know about how your family has changed this past year?*

Kelly: Yeah, it's hard to change your family sometimes. Like, I have two friends whose parents got divorced, and I have one friend who had a brother who was born with Down syndrome. These things kind of change how your family is, and it's hard. It takes a long time for it to feel normal again, and even then it will never be the same. I guess it's part of growing up, but it doesn't feel so good. It helps to know Jesus loves me still, and it helps to pray, but that doesn't make it feel better.

Care and Counseling Tips

THE BASICS

Today's family faces myriad complex challenges. In any given family, there is rarely a time when something is not in flux. But God can use these very family crises to bring families closer together, create bonds that are stronger than before, and heal wounds that have been left untreated for a long time. It's important to know how the changing tides in the family affect the children who are tossed and turned by the waves these changes cause.

Change in the family takes many forms. For one child, change may be the reality of a mother or father leaving the family to serve in the military thousands of miles away, knowing that this parent may not return. For another child, it may be a parent losing a job, forcing the family to move into a smaller home where there will be significantly fewer packages under the Christmas tree. In some children, it may come after just having weathered the storm of a divorce and a stepparent and stepsiblings move in. For yet another, it may be an added sibling from an adoption.

No matter the cause, you can help children adapt to these often traumatic and overwhelming changes in the family by offering a constant in their lives: a place of love and long-term spiritual growth.

Care Tips

Because each family change is unique, there really is no one best way to help children through family crises. The good news is there are several things you can do in any major change that will help children move through the initial shock to adaptation and spiritual growth.

+ Practice authenticity.

Children facing change in the family already feel abandoned and unheard, so they are keenly attuned to whether or not others *truly* care. You can help by putting aside other concerns of the moment and focusing on the needs of the child. Actively listen as the child shares feelings, concerns, and even resentment. Spend time together doing what the child likes to do. One-on-one time such as a trip to an ice-cream shop, time at the playground, or throwing a baseball in the park can help a child know you care about him or her as an individual. Connecting through the child's interests will help you build a relationship the child sees as a constant amid painful change.

+ Tell the truth.

Children have numerous questions as they face family change and crisis: Why? What did I do wrong? What does this mean for me? What's next? While it's tempting to comfort them with pat answers, the best thing you can do is admit that you don't know all the answers and be consistently honest.

As they struggle through major changes, children will depend on you for consistency and follow-through. It's critical to live up to promises—even the small ones. If you promise to talk to a child after church, be sure to be available to do so. Every promise you keep, however small, will build a child's trust in you.

+ Accept the child.

When children are going through family crises, let them know that it's

OK to be angry and sad. Change is difficult, especially for children who may not grasp the underlying reasons for the change. Allowing children to express their feelings will give them a safe place to talk and be honest.

WHEN TO REFER

Most changes can be handled through constant love and attention. But some instances require help from licensed counselors:

+ When there is danger of harm to self or others.

If anyone is in danger from lashing out in response to anger or resentment, help the family find professional help. You may also need to warn others in danger or local law enforcement if safety becomes an issue.

+ When there is suspected child or elder abuse.

Some family changes come as a result of harmful relationships marked by physical, sexual, or emotional abuse. If you notice signs of abuse (see Chapter 1), you may be required to report it to authorities. Check with your church's child safety policy or local authorities.

+ When any mental health issue is discovered where you don't have appropriate professional training to respond.

When a child shows uncharacteristically slow adaptation, you may want to consider professional help.

Counseling Tips

Counseling a family through change will not only guide the family through the changing dynamics, but it will also help the family grow stronger in the long run. As you counsel the family, do your best to understand the change the family is going through and all the feelings associated with it.

✛ Teach the family new skills.

Caring for families in crisis should be a process by which the family learns skills they can apply to future changes and situations. As you work with the family through their challenges, help them grow in these areas:

• *Time with God*—Help families arrange a specific time to read and talk about God's Word. Suggest a simple devotional book that explores Scripture and asks life-application questions. As family members become better acquainted with God's Word, they'll become better acquainted with God's loving and unchanging nature.

• *Budgeting*—Many family crises are a result of (or lead to) financial problems. Helping the family find ways to effectively manage money will give them a foundation to face future financial issues.

• *Family meetings*—As families work through changes, it's important that they find time to strategically communicate and work as a team. Help families arrange a weekly time to meet together to bring up issues, talk about concerns, and share their ideas without fear of judgment or being ignored.

✛ Identify and challenge assumptions.

Unexpected changes in the family, such as the loss of a job, a family member leaving, or financial stress, can often create a variety of assumptions. For example, a child might say, "Mommy doesn't love me, because she's gone all the time." This is based on the assumption that if the mother did love the child, she wouldn't be traveling on business trips every other week. In this example, clarifying the financial needs of the family, the reasons the parents made the choices they did, and possible other options can help the child challenge this assumption. It's important to identify assumptions, assess their validity, and help all family members respond lovingly and effectively.

+ Facilitate family communication.

Modeling and facilitating honest, clear, relevant communication can be very helpful in counseling families through major change. God often uses crisis situations to help families that have fallen into a pattern of living separate lives to remember the value of a family dinner together or an opportunity to listen to a family member's heart. You can help families grow closer by challenging them to develop specific communication skills, such as active listening, sharing deeper feelings and issues, and talking together through difficult challenges.

SCRIPTURE HELP

+ **2 Samuel 22:2**
+ **Psalm 46:1**
+ **Psalm 46:10**
+ **Proverbs 14:26**
+ **Matthew 12:46-50**

+ **Matthew 18:21-22**
+ **Luke 10:30-37**
+ **Romans 12:10**
+ **1 Corinthians 13:13**
+ **2 Corinthians 9:14**

Additional Care Tips

The feelings of loneliness, anxiety, and tension in changing families are difficult for children to deal with daily. You can help the child and family work through major family changes by providing a constant in your ministry. First Corinthians 13:13 reminds us to be consistent in faith, hope, and love. Keep these three things in mind as you minister to children and families affected by major change.

+ Promote a ministry of faith in God during times of change.

Christ remains steadfast when the plans we had for our lives are destroyed. You can provide concrete ways for children and families to connect to God when they feel afraid or worry that God isn't with them. Here are a few practical ways to do this:

• Encourage families to spend some devotional time on examples of how God stood by families in the Bible during times of crisis (Abraham and Isaac, Joseph, and Mary and Joseph with Jesus).

• Ask family members to think about times in their lives when they felt overwhelmed and to write down the ways they felt God's presence during those times. Then encourage them to look for those assurances in the present change.

• Talk to children about what they know is true about God. Then encourage hurting children to remember that God will never change, even when everything else seems to be changing.

+ Create an atmosphere of hope for children and families.

When children are going through major change in the family, they can find hope in looking forward to small things. Make plans to spend one-on-one time with a child, doing things he or she wants to do. These plans will give hope for something exciting in the future. A stack of cards from friends or small occasional gifts can also provide some hope in a time of major change.

+ Create a climate of love.

When children face changes that scare them, they need to know they're loved. Many major changes, such as a loved one leaving, family financial difficulties, or a new parental figure in the home, can cause children to question this. Helping a child feel loved can be as simple as telling the child how special he or she is. It's a good idea to designate a leader in your ministry as someone who makes it a point to care for a child affected by a major change. An adult mentor or friend can be very helpful in providing hope and love to a child who needs a constant person he or she can look up to.

+ Empower the family.

Encourage and empower the family to help provide the love and hope the child needs to grow in faith. Team up with parents to help children work through the difficult situation. Offer support, but encourage them to intentionally make time to show love to their children.

ADDITIONAL RESOURCES

+ Books

The Family: A Christian Perspective on the Contemporary Home. Jack Balswick and Judith Balswick. Grand Rapids, MI: Baker Publishing Group, 2007.

The Problem of Pain. C.S. Lewis. Harper San Francisco, a division of Harper Collins Publishers; New Ed edition, 2001.

+ Online Resources

www.family.org (Focus on the Family)
www.familylife.com (Family Life: A Division of Campus Crusade for Christ)

What Not to Say

As children go through major change, they need to know that it will be OK. There are things you can say to help them know this. But there are some things that can hinder.

+ "Everyone goes through change. You'll get over it."
This statement can make children feel guilty for the changes the family is facing or the emotions they are experiencing. Your role is to build a foundation of faith, hope, and love.

+ "Don't be so selfish."
Feeling loss for "the way it used to be" is not selfish. These words will only shut the door to honest evaluation of true feelings and remove any possible growth or adapting to the new situation.

+ "Jesus wants us to love everyone."
Children know God wants them to love, but life is tough at times and they need to know it's OK to be honest about their feelings. They need to know Jesus loves them even when they aren't perfect.

+ "You have to forgive."
In time they will. But right now they need some comfort and understanding. They need to be allowed to express what's on their hearts. Once they're secure in God's love and your acceptance, then they will feel the freedom to forgive the changes that have been forced upon them.

+ "If you pray, God will make it all go away."
This is a promise you can't deliver. It's true that God answers prayer. But the pain seldom just "goes away." If a child is told that all he or she has to do is ask God to take away the pain, and it doesn't happen, what will happen to the hope and faith he or she had developed up to that point?

Don't promise a child something that human beings don't have the ability to deliver.

What to Say

+ "It's OK to feel _____."

Validating and accepting a child's feelings during times of change in the family is extremely important. The child needs to know that it's OK to be angry, sad, or frightened, and that he or she won't be judged for those feelings. The more a child realizes he or she can share true feelings, the less overwhelming those emotions become.

+ "I'm here for you."

Knowing children can come to you and be honest about the pain they are experiencing is such a gift. Knowing they can be real without being judged allows them to face the realities of their situation and to take courage that they can go on.

+ "I'd like to pray."

We belong to a big God. One who is able to hear our complaints and to strengthen and grow us through the change process. Always pray with the child as well as telling the child you will continue to pray for him or her. This gives the opportunity for you to model how to bring our deepest and most real feelings to a God who can do something about them.

+ "I care about you."

This shows that you offer a constant loving relationship the child can rely on. Despite how scared or angry a child might feel, he or she can always know that your love is always there, no matter what the future may hold.

CHAPTER FOUR

Death
Walking Through the Grieving Process With Children

with counseling insights from **SHAUNA SKILLERN, LMFT**
+ care tips from **HEATHER DUNN**

Randy is a middle child in his family. He has two older sisters who no longer live at home, and a younger brother. Randy was in fifth grade when his dad was diagnosed with cancer. His dad lived a fairly normal life for the first year after the diagnosis. After that, he had more intense chemotherapy and stayed at home for six months until he was moved to a hospice care facility for the last month of his life. Randy's mom cared for his dad, as well as home-schooled Randy and his brother, who was in second grade. The family continued their involvement in their church, and the church provided as much support as they could.

Comforting Children in Crisis: *Randy, how did you feel when you first found out your dad had cancer?*

Randy: I didn't really understand what was going to happen. I was scared mostly because everyone around me was scared and sad. I knew I had to be strong for my mom and dad and little brother.

CCC: *What was hardest for you?*

Randy: I really didn't like people always telling me how sorry they were for me. It just made me feel worse.

CCC: *What did you want people to do?*

Randy: I don't know. I just didn't like all of the sympathy. It felt like everyone was watching me with these sad eyes. I guess it would have been nice if someone would have said, "I'm really sorry. I'm putting $50,000 in an account for you. When you're ready to go to college or really need something, let me know." That couldn't really happen, but it would have been nice.

CCC: *Were you worried about money?*

Randy: We didn't have much money, so yes, I guess I was.

CCC: *What was your biggest worry?*

Randy: If we would have food. My dad had always gone to work so we'd have food and money to pay for things. He wasn't able to work anymore, so I worried about how we'd get money for food.

CCC: *What was the best thing anyone did for you?*

Randy: Someone threw me a birthday party. I don't know who it was, but it was great. My mom couldn't have done it, but she got the credit for it. She actually looked happy, which was nice. There was cake and ice cream and friends from church with presents. We played games, and there were treats for my friends to take home. It was something I didn't expect would happen, so it was really surprising.

CCC: *How did you feel the first weeks after your dad died?*

Randy: I felt nothing and then I felt everything. First I just didn't feel anything. I just watched things happen and did what I was supposed to. At least I think I did. I was numb. Then I felt overwhelmed. I was relieved because now my mom could pay some attention to me, but then I felt guilty for wanting attention when she was so sad. I'd get excited thinking about my dad, but then I'd remember he was dead. Then I'd feel really lonely. I felt mad that it happened to my dad—and to me. It didn't seem right when I had fun, but I was tired of always being sad. I wanted to be happy but didn't feel like it would be right to be happy when I was supposed to be sad. I was on this giant roller coaster. It was really hard, and at the time, I couldn't have described it to you.

CCC: *And then what?*

Randy: I think I got tired of all of the emotions, so I just checked out. I didn't want to feel, so I pretended everything was just fine. I tried not to stand out so people wouldn't ask me about my feelings. I smiled most of the time. I made sure I was always with someone who did lots of talking so I wouldn't have to. I pretty much kept everything inside.

CCC: *How did that work for you?*

Randy: It got me through for a while. It probably wasn't the best way to deal with things, though. I made it through middle school that way. High school, though, was different. I don't know if it was because I was numb and wanted to feel again or whether I had too much pain and wanted to allow it to escape. Whatever. I started cutting my wrists. I didn't want to die, really. I let certain people know, I guess for the attention, or maybe so I wouldn't hurt myself too badly. I can't explain it all, really. I knew it wasn't a good thing to do, but I did it anyway. I got lots of attention and finally worked through things. I don't do it anymore.

CCC: *Where was God through all of this?*

Randy: Sometimes I knew he was there. Someone put groceries on our porch just when we needed them; someone threw me a birthday party. Those kinds of things reminded me that God was there. Other times, I felt like God was totally gone. I'd cry out to him and there would just be nothing. I wanted him to heal my dad and bring him back to life. That didn't happen. It kind of shakes your faith when you trust someone and they don't come through. I still don't know why my dad had to die, but I know God has his reasons. I'm back to trusting God—most of the time, anyway.

CCC: *Looking back, what was most helpful to you?*

Randy: A lot of people really tried to help me. One person sat down with me when I was worried about what would happen next and helped me remember all the times God had provided for me in the past. We talked about whether God would disappear now. That was good. A teacher asked me to write a paper about facing the death of my dad. I had to read it to the class. It was one of the hardest things I did, but it was also one of the most helpful. My teacher stood right next to me and helped me some when I was too choked up to speak. When I was having my hard times in high school, a couple of the youth leaders from church were really there for me. They called me and checked on me and held me accountable.

CCC: *What would you tell others who are facing a death in the family?*

Randy: It's not going to be fun, but you'll get through it. Tell people what you want and don't want. Be real, and don't hide it.

Care and Counseling Tips

THE BASICS

Grief is a very painful emotion, and it can be difficult to see a child hurting. Because of this, adults often try to shield children from the intense emotions that surround the loss of a loved one. But like adults, children need the opportunity to grieve. They experience the same stages of grief as adults, but these stages do not have to go in a certain order or follow a specific timeline. The grief process can range anywhere from a month to several years.

However, children do grieve differently from adults. While adults tend to grieve for an extended period of time, children tend to go in and out of the grieving process because they don't have the ability to deal with those big feelings on a consistent basis. Here are three of the most basic stages of grief, and how children handle them:

- *Shock and disbelief*—thinking "this can't be true," making comments that a family member will be back soon, asking questions about death.
- *Extreme feelings*—anger, sadness, aggression, tearfulness, having difficulty concentrating, lashing out at people close to them because they don't understand their intense feelings.
- *Acceptance*—starting to move forward without frequent thoughts of the death, returning to normal activities, sharing positive memories of their loved one rather than focusing on their sad feelings.

Children understand death differently at various ages. Here are some ideas for how a child's age affects his or her understanding of the finality of death:

- *Under 6 years old:* Most children under 6 won't be able to understand what it means to never see someone again. They might say, "Is Grandma going to be dead tomorrow?" They will probably ask repetitive questions about what death is in an attempt to understand it.
- *6 to 8 years old:* At this age, children start to gain a greater

understanding of death, but often think on a fantasy level. They may develop a fear of ghosts and see death as a scary thing. They may show signs of guilt, feeling like they somehow caused the death. They may also display fear that others around them will die.

• *9 years old to teenager:* Children will now start to fully understand the finality of death. While they can express their feelings more verbally, they may not choose to initially. At this age, they want to feel accepted by their friends, pastors, teachers, and coaches—if a parent dies, they may feel different from their friends. Encourage kids this age that their feelings are accepted and normal.

SCRIPTURE HELP

+ **Psalm 23**
+ **Psalm 121**
+ **Proverbs 3:5-6**
+ **Ecclesiastes 3:1-8**
+ **Jeremiah 31:13**

+ **Matthew 7:7-11**
+ **John 14:1-4**
+ **Romans 8:26-28**
+ **Philippians 4:8**
+ **Philippians 4:12-13**

ADDITIONAL RESOURCES

+ **Books**

How to Talk to Your Kids About Really Important Things. Charles E. Schaefer and Theresa F. DiGeronimo. San Francisco, CA: Jossey-Bass Publishers, 1994.

Helping Children Cope with Death. Portland, OR: The Dougy Center, 1997.

When Dinosaurs Die: A Guide to Understanding Death. Laurie K. Brown and Marc Brown. Boston: Little, Brown, and Company, 1996.

Care Tips

+ Encourage active grieving.

The healthiest way to grieve is by active grieving, where a person spends time trying to live a normal daily life while still devoting time to expressing feelings of sadness. Adults may spend long periods in active grieving. Children, however, will display brief spurts of sadness or anger. The rest of the time they may want to play or go about their daily routine. This doesn't mean they don't care— it's normal! The average intense grieving period for a child is eight to ten months, but, obviously, a child will feel the effects of the loss for a long time after that.

+ Be there.

Help children and their families feel cared for. Just knowing that you're there to help will make a big difference. Be available to the grieving family, and follow their lead in finding ways to help.

+ Listen.

It's helpful for a grieving child to have someone outside the family to talk to. Don't judge or feel like you have to give advice—just listen. In any given conversation, the child may or may not want to talk about the death. Be available to listen to whatever the child wants to talk about.

+ Help with daily chores.

The details of daily life can be overwhelming to a grieving family. Take them dinner, offer to pick the kids up from school, spend time with the children while the family is making funeral arrangements. The family may not feel comfortable asking for help, so don't wait for an invitation. Think of a few practical things you could do for the family, and then offer.

+ Show love.

Death can make children feel insecure and frightened. If you know the family well, give the child a loving hug. If a hug isn't appropriate, a gentle pat on the shoulder and a few kind words can help the child feel less isolated.

+ Pray.

Pray with and for the family. Let them know that others are praying for them, too. Even if the family feels too overwhelmed, or even too angry, to pray for themselves, they'll know that others are caring for them on a spiritual level.

HELPING A FAMILY WITH THE LOSS OF A CHILD

Experiencing the death of a child is a tragic loss. The family will need extra care and understanding from the church.

A family that loses a child may experience anger toward God. The best thing to do is to offer nonjudgmental support as they work through their feelings. As a church, pray often for the family and let them know they're in your prayers.

If they're open to it, pray *with* the family. It can be healing for them to participate spiritually, but it could be a comfort to let someone else take the lead.

Counseling Tips

+ Offer nonverbal ways to express feelings.
Many children aren't able to express their feelings verbally. Offer crayons, puppets, and dolls to help kids use the language of play.

+ Maintain routine and structure.
Children feel safe when they know what is going to happen during the day. But after a death, life feels unpredictable. Encourage the family to maintain a comforting routine for the child, and offer to help. Take the child to school, church, and sports practices. Help the child get back into a daily routine that feels safe and predictable.

+ Discuss heaven.
Explain the hope of heaven to the child. Comfort the child with the reminder that we will see loved ones in heaven one day. Talk with the child about a loved one living with Jesus, even though we can't see that person.

+ Allow the child to help.
Most people, including children, experience a sense of helplessness after the death of a family member. Ask the child to help with little things, such as making sure the dog gets water or saying a prayer at dinner every day. Having a small task to do on a regular basis will help the child feel more in control.

+ Give a comfort token.
Give the child a special stone or stuffed animal to carry as a reminder of God's presence and love.

+ Create a goodbye ritual.
It's helpful to let the child attend the funeral. If that's not feasible, help the family create a goodbye ritual that the child can understand. An example

might be burying a loved one's possession in the backyard, putting a good-bye message to Dad inside a balloon that the child can watch fly into the air, or drawing a goodbye picture that the child can leave at church.

+ Allow the child to play.

Children grieve differently from adults, and will probably have short bursts of sadness followed by times where they just want to forget about the death and play. Allow this time. It's important not to ignore the death, but don't expect a grieving child to want to talk about it all the time.

WHEN TO REFER

It's common for a child to experience problems for several months after the death of a loved one. A child may have difficulties in school or be more "clingy" with a parent. Be on the lookout for behaviors that signal depression, such as a loss of interest in activities, aggression, thoughts about death, social withdrawal, difficulty concentrating, or loss of energy.

All of these symptoms are normal shortly after losing a loved one. However, if five or more symptoms continue for a month or longer, refer the child to a professional counselor. If the child has frequent nightmares, intense mood swings, or suicidal thoughts, refer him or her for professional assistance immediately.

Additional Care Tips

After a death, it's important to support a grieving family. Here are some helpful ideas that church members can do.

+ Work together on tasks.
Take turns helping the family with daily tasks. Create a schedule to provide meals for the family. Run errands or transport kids to soccer practice and school. Offer child care so the adults can grieve or take care of arrangements.

+ Visit, if the family wants company.
The family may feel lonely and isolated after their loss. Help minimize the impact of this by having members of the church visit the family often—but only if the family *wants* visitors. Develop a schedule for who can be available to call or go over when the family desires visitors. Choose families with same-age children in case the mourning child wants to play. But be sensitive if family members would rather be left alone to concentrate on and comfort each other.

+ Create a group card.
Have all the kids in your ministry create and sign a card to send to a grieving friend. After a death in the family, a child may not make it to church as often as usual. Such a child will appreciate knowing that he or she is thought of and missed. This idea also gives the children in your church the opportunity to help someone they care about.

+ Pray.
Offer the children in your ministry the opportunity to pray together for the hurting child. Encourage the children to pray on their own as well.

What Not to Say

+ "You're the man of the house now."

After the death of a parent, a child often feels a sense of responsibility for surviving family members. It's common for children to try to follow all the rules and do extra chores because they don't want to be another cause of stress. They may even try to take on more responsibility than they can handle. Saying "You're the man of the house now" or "Take care of your mommy" only reinforces the unrealistic notion that it's the child's job to take care of the family. Allow the child to mourn in an age-appropriate fashion, and dissuade the child from trying to take on adult responsibilities.

+ "I heard you lost your mommy."

It's hard for children to understand death, so it's important to use clear words such as *death* and *dead* to keep kids from getting confused. If they hear phrases like *left us* or *lost* they may take the words literally and think that mommy can be found or that she left intentionally.

+ "He's in a better place now."

While the phrase may be true, it may make the child feel as though there was something wrong with their home or the care that was provided. A child may even think that he or she somehow contributed to unhappiness or problems that made their home less than ideal. It's OK to talk about heaven with the child, just remember that they may be worried that God will take them there soon, too.

+ "It's time to move on with your life."

Everyone moves through the grieving process at different rates. One thing a grieving child doesn't need is more guilt—even if it's been a year or two since the death. Suggest ideas to help the child continue processing the loss, and then help him or her implement the ideas. For example, build a memory garden together or help someone else who is grieving.

What to Say

+ "It's OK to cry."

Children don't know how to deal with strong emotions. Letting them know that those emotions are normal and that it's OK to express them will help them grieve.

+ "I remember when your dad and I used to go fishing."

Remind the child of the good things about the family member. Help the child reminisce about his or her own fond memories of the loved one.

+ "What do you miss most?"

Help a child share feelings by asking clear questions that can't be answered with a simple yes or no. For example, instead of asking, "Do you miss your brother?" ask instead, "What was your favorite thing to do with your brother?" This will give the child a starting place to sort out his or her feelings.

+ "I don't know what to say, but I'm here for you."

If you don't know what to say, admit it. You can't take away the child's pain, but you can let him or her know that you care and want to help. The most important gift you can give is listening.

+ "He loved you so much."

A grieving child longs for the loving touches and words that are now missing. Remind the child of how much the deceased loved him or her, and recall times you saw that love in action.

+ "Let's go get ice cream."

Help the child find a bit of normalcy. Don't have an agenda, but be willing to listen if he or she wants to talk. Otherwise, just have a quiet time together. Ask about school, friends, or pets. Sometimes it's nice just to think or talk about something other than the loss.

CHAPTER FIVE

Depression

Supporting Children in the Darkness

with counseling insights from JANNA KINNER, MSW
+ care tips from LARRY SHALLENBERGER

I parked in the hospital lot and took the well-worn path to the fourth floor. I pressed the round silver button on the wall next to the placard that read "Behavioral Health." After a moment, a buzzer sounded and the steel doors opened.

I entered, signed in at the nursing station, and took a seat in the visitation room. A few moments later, Claire padded into the room, wearing hospital-issued robe and slippers.

Claire fidgeted with the robe-tie in her hands. I looked down and noticed the fresh cut marks on her wrists. Last night Claire had locked herself in the bathroom and tried to cut her wrists with a piece of broken glass. The wounds on her wrists were superficial. Even so, her mother took no chances and called 911. This wasn't Claire's first suicidal gesture, and it wasn't her first hospitalization—and Claire was only in fourth grade. Despite her age, she had many reasons to be experiencing depression.

Claire lived with her single mother and a younger brother with special needs. Claire's brother had an assortment of physical and mental problems that clamored for their mother's limited time and resources. Claire's mother was constantly shuttling between work and the children's hospital.

Between those trips and her own issues with depression, Claire's mom had little energy left for her daughter.

Claire's father was in a prison five states away. Claire had never met him and had never been told why he was in prison. Claire filled her vacuum of information with idealized pictures of her father. Everything would be fine if she could just live with him.

This wasn't the first time that Claire and I had sat across from each other, trying to deal with her depression. I'd talked to her before about the importance of talking to someone about her sad feelings and the anger she felt toward her mom. As I sat with her now, I tried to break the ice.

"Pretty boring here, huh?"

"Uh-huh. I can't do anything. But still, it's better than being at home."

"You're only going to be here for a few more days, Claire. How are you going to use your time?"

"What do you mean?"

"Claire, you have some choices to make. It's not a sin to be sad. And it's not a sin, even, to be mad at your mom. A lot of people suffer from depression. Some get depressed because of bad things that happen to them. And some people get depressed, well, because they're just born with a tendency to feel sad. And some people have both. It's not your fault that you feel sad and angry, but you need to come up with a plan for how you're going to handle those emotions."

Claire stopped smiling. "I'm taking my medicine. But I hate how it makes me feel."

"Keep taking your medicine. That's good. That's a big part of taking care of yourself. I want to keep you around. But you also need to talk with a counselor about your feelings. You're going to need to learn how to talk to your mother about what's bugging you."

That was too much. Claire lowered her head and crossed her arms.

I changed the topic by making fun of the hospital food with Claire. Once the tension had passed, I probed again. "What is your case manager asking you to do when you get out of here?"

"Oh, she says that I need therapy by myself and that I also need to go to counseling with my mom. I'll talk to a counselor. But not with my mom in the room."

I sat silently across from Claire. I didn't want to push too hard and make her close down again. Finally I said, "Claire, your sad and angry feelings are like oily rags sitting too close to a furnace. They caught fire last night. You tried to hurt yourself. I don't want that to happen again. There are a lot of things you can't control. You can't control that your brother is sick or that your dad is in prison. It's not your fault that your mom is so busy—"

"—*Don't* talk about my mother!" Claire shot a scowl.

I looked at my watch.

"OK. It's almost time for me to go. So let me make this offer. You or your mom are allowed to invite me to be a part of your treatment team. If you want, I can sit on the planning team with your counselor, your psychiatrist, your teachers. And you're old enough to be a part of the team, too."

"What's the team do?"

"The team works together to help you meet your goal. Say you decide that you don't want to feel sad and angry anymore—the team would help you make a plan to change that."

"Why would you be on the team?"

"Well, God can be a big part of helping you feel better. I can teach you how to talk to God about your problems. And because Jesus forgives us, I can help you learn how to forgive the people who have disappointed you. But you don't need to decide that today. Think about it. I'll call you when you get back home."

We hugged and I passed through the steel doors again. I heard the click of the lock, and I prayed that God would help Claire choose to cope with her depression.

Care and Counseling Tips

THE BASICS

Depression is a serious mood disorder that can feel painful and isolating for those in its grips. Depression affects how kids feel and behave in all environments—at school, at home, at church, and with friends. Since it can also be accompanied by other mood or behavior problems, parents and ministry leaders may at first feel overwhelmed when trying to help a depressed child. But don't give up! By sharing the problem and caring in practical ways, you can help relieve the oppressive symptoms of depression.

+ Understand the symptoms.

Depression can be better understood by paying attention to four aspects of a child's functioning:

Thoughts: The child views him- or herself as worthless or as a failure, has problems concentrating, and/or has thoughts of suicide.

Feelings: The child feels sad or irritable nearly every day for several weeks, and/or doesn't enjoy activities that used to be pleasurable.

Behavior: The child acts restless and fidgety, or acts sluggish, tired, and unmotivated.

Body functions: The child experiences weight gain or loss, and/or sleeps too much or not enough.

+ Understand the causes.

There is no one cause of depression. Sometimes stressful events such as moving, divorce, birth of a sibling, or a death in the family can trigger depression. Many mental health professionals agree that there are also genetic, biochemical, and hormonal factors involved. Plus, negative thinking can cause or perpetuate feelings of worthlessness and isolation.

+ Watch for coexisting mood problems.

In children, depression often occurs with other mood disorders, such as anxiety disorders, separation anxiety, bipolar disorder, conduct disorder, obsessive-compulsive disorder, or other emotional or behavioral problems. A mental health professional can help the family address all of the symptoms the child is experiencing.

SCRIPTURE HELP

+ **Psalm 42:5**
+ **Psalm 146**
+ **Isaiah 40:31**
+ **Lamentations 3:19-26**
+ **Romans 8:37-39**

+ **2 Corinthians 1:8-11**
+ **Philippians 4:6**
+ **Philippians 4:8**
+ **Hebrews 12:12-13**
+ **1 John 4:18a**

Care Tips

Childhood depression often goes unidentified, especially in preschool children. When you suspect that a child in your ministry is struggling with depression, no matter what the child's age, address your concerns right away.

+ Confront aggression.

Some children who experience depression act out aggressively—either verbally or physically. The attack might be targeted at him- or herself (self-deprecating remarks and/or cutting or scratching), another person (kicking, hitting, or antagonizing others), or objects (slamming doors, punching walls).

You are responsible for creating a safe environment for *all* of the children involved in your ministry. Don't accept aggression. Firmly tell the aggressive child that his or her behavior is unacceptable, and suggest appropriate ways to act. If the aggression continues, remove the child from the situation until you can create a safety plan with the child's parents.

+ Confront isolation.

Depression can be deepened by feeling lonely or cut off from others. So create a ministry of acceptance and inclusion. Teach your kids how to make introductions, welcome newcomers, and practice hospitality. Help shy children become involved in activities. Partner children with kids they don't know to encourage new friendships.

+ Confront suicidal thoughts.

One of the scariest experiences you may have as a ministry leader is hearing one of your children mention suicide. Many people shy away from talking about suicide because they're afraid they might plant an idea in a child's head. This is a myth—asking about self-harm won't make a child suicidal if he or she isn't already.

Directly ask, "Are you feeling like hurting yourself or committing suicide?" Express genuine concern for the child, and don't agree to keep secrets. Get help immediately by calling the National Suicide Prevention Lifeline at 1-800-273-TALK (8255) or 911.

MEDICATION

Many mental health professionals agree that medication in conjunction with therapy can help children suffering from severe depression. Encourage the child's parents to openly discuss any medication questions or concerns they may have with their child's psychiatrist.

Counseling Tips

Depression often calls for a professional counselor (see the When to Refer box on page 65). However, you can continue to support the child and his or her family during the journey to recovery.

+ Teach thought-stopping.

Depressed kids often make self-deprecating remarks such as "No one likes me," "I'm worthless because I keep messing up," and "I'm not good enough." A child might also become excessively worried about things beyond his or her control.

Challenge these negative patterns by teaching "thought-stopping." Begin by defining the child's specific remarks that concern you, and then ask the child if you can point out such remarks in the future. Make a game of saying "Stop!" and holding up your hand when the child makes the negative remarks. Help the child see and stop the negative patterns that exist in his or her thinking.

Once an older child is able to recognize these negative patterns, suggest that the child put a picture of a stop sign in his or her room at home, or in a school notebook. Having a visual reminder to stop negative thinking will reinforce new, more positive thought patterns.

+ Work with the family.

Many mental health professionals agree that mood disorders tend to run in families. If you recognize that the child's parents or other family members have symptoms of depression or another mood disorder, discuss your concerns with the family and refer them to a licensed family counselor.

Children with depression often have problems sleeping (too much or too little) and eating (loss of appetite or overeating). Encourage the family to create a routine for the child, with regular bedtimes and healthy eating habits. Consistency will help the child get back on track.

+ Set a positive example.

Establish yourself as a trustworthy person to talk to. Make a point to listen carefully and nonjudgmentally to the kids in your ministry. Affirm all of your children, and remind them that they are made in God's image.

+ Take care of yourself.

Working with a child who is depressed can be physically, emotionally, and mentally draining. Don't shoulder the burden alone—involve others in caring for the child and family.

WHEN TO REFER

Parents should consider seeking help from a Christian licensed mental health professional:

+ When the child's daily functioning is impaired.

If the child is unable to get out of bed, eat, groom, or bathe, get help.

+ When the child is at risk of hurting him- or herself.

If the child engages in self-harm behaviors such as cutting, biting, or scratching, get help.

+ When the child is a danger to others.

If the child expresses a desire to harm another person, immediately notify the child's parents and refer the child to a mental healthcare worker. Also, notify the person he or she has plans to harm.

+ When a child discloses that he or she is considering suicide, *ALWAYS* get help right away.

Don't leave the child alone. Together, call the National Suicide Prevention Lifeline (1-800-273-TALK). If he or she is unwilling to talk to someone, you can call 911 for an emergency response team.

Additional Care Tips

+ Grieve as a group.

Sad events, such as death or divorce, can trigger depression in kids. Almost every child has experienced a loss of some kind—even if it's the loss of a pet. It's normal for these life experiences to be depressing. Resist the urge to gloss over difficult subjects, and don't be afraid to address the topic of grief in your ministry. By normalizing the grief process, you'll help children understand that being sad is a natural feeling.

Then teach your kids that they can find their true joy in Jesus. Try activities such as writing problems on index cards, then attaching the cards to a wooden cross or ripping the cards up after a prayer. You could also lead children in writing letters to God about how they feel about their losses.

+ Be persistent.

Kids who struggle with depression may not feel like joining in group events, even activities they've enjoyed in the past. It can feel overwhelming to have to get out of bed and join happy children. Don't give up—keep trying to include the depressed child in your activities. Being with others helps battle the isolation of depression.

+ Assign a mentor or partner.

When kids are acting out aggressively or irritably in your ministry, they may be asking for some extra attention. Designate an adult or teen to offer one-on-one attention during your ministry meeting times. Not only can this mentor model positive interactions with other kids, he or she can also address some of the child's problematic behaviors quietly, before they disrupt the whole group.

+ Promote a healthy lifestyle.

Kids who are depressed often lack the motivation to exercise—but research shows that exercise and healthy eating can help alleviate the symptoms of depression. So make sure your ministry is active! Play fun, noncompetitive games outside on a nice day, and serve only wholesome snacks.

ADDITIONAL RESOURCES

+ Books

Raising a Moody Child: How to Cope With Depression and Bipolar Disorder. Mary A. Fristad, Ph.D., and Jill S. Goldberg Arnold, Ph.D. New York: The Guilford Press, 2004.

The Childhood Depression Sourcebook. Jeffrey A. Miller, Ph.D. Lincolnwood, IL: Lowell House, 1998.

The Depressed Child: A Parent's Guide for Rescuing Kids. Dr. Douglas A. Riley. Dallas: Taylor Publishing Company, 2001.

+ Online Resources

www.aacap.org (American Academy of Child and Adolescent Psychiatry)

www.medicinenet.com/depression_in_children/article.htm (Medicine Net)

What Not to Say

+ "Maybe you need to get right with God."

Yes, sometimes depression is the result of guilt and unconfessed sin. However that's not always, or even *often,* the case. You run the risk of communicating to the child that his or her sadness is the result of a bad relationship with God. And this will only discourage the child further.

+ "You don't need medicine if you've got God."

We'd never say that to a diabetic, would we? But for some reason, some Christians mistakenly see depression as strictly a spiritual problem and not as a medical condition.

+ "Sure, we can keep this just between us."

Don't agree to keep secrets, especially if a child mentions suicide. *Always* take such comments seriously. Don't leave the child alone. Together call the National Suicide Prevention Lifeline (1-800-273-TALK). If he or she is unwilling to talk to someone, call 911 for an emergency response team.

Explain that you have the child's best interest in mind at all times.

+ "You're one messed-up kid."

Learn to separate the mood disorder from the child. Help parents get in this habit, too—if they have been living with difficult behaviors for a long time, it might be hard for them to imagine their child without depression. Focus on the positive, and point out the child's strengths.

+ "Just think positive."

This statement doesn't take into account the child's feelings and worries. Positive thinking is something to work toward, but it isn't an automatic fix. Listen nonjudgmentally, and include the child and family in formulating practical solutions.

What to Say

+ "Sometimes I get really sad, too."

A depressed child needs to know that it's normal for everyone, even adults, to feel sad. You can model healthy emotional responses by telling a child of a time when you were very sad and how you handled those emotions.

+ "Jesus felt sad."

The Bible says that Jesus was very sad once (Matthew 26:36-38). A depressed child can find comfort in knowing that even Jesus struggled with strong negative emotions.

+ "Are you feeling suicidal?"

Even if the child is in professional counseling, don't be afraid to continue checking in on how he or she is feeling. By being upfront in asking this question, you're opening a door for the child to trust you if he or she does need help. If not, you won't be planting an idea that isn't there.

+ "What can you do to make this situation better?"

Sometimes the negative statements that children with depression make (such as "No one will ever like me") can sound like complaining—and constantly hearing complaints is draining. Instead of just ignoring these comments, ask the child to think of a positive solution. This will help the child to shift his or her thinking toward improving the situation.

+ "I love you, and God loves you, too."

This may seem simplistic, but sometimes kids who struggle with depression lose sight of the fact that people really do care. Even more important, this statement also reminds the child that God is present and loving.

CHAPTER SIX

Divorce
Encouraging Children in Brokenness

with counseling insights from **LINDA SWINDELL, PH.D.**
+ care tips from **BECKI MANNI**

Luke was normally such a quiet little boy in Sunday school. He played with blocks while the class filled up each week, and then he sat as close to his sister, Emily, as possible. He watched others sing during praise time and answered questions when called on, but he rarely participated on his own. He was 5 and Emily was 7, and they were inseparable.

But this week things were different. As Brenda devoted her attention to the new family dropping off a child, suddenly a block whizzed past her head. Screams came from the play area at the back of the room. Luke threw blocks and screamed at Jason for knocking down his tower. Emily tried in vain to calm her brother's outburst, but Luke seemed inconsolable. Tears streamed down both their faces as Brenda entered the fray.

She quickly wrapped one arm around Luke and the other around his tearful sister. All the while she struggled to figure out what could possibly have started the chaos in her normally orderly room. Neither child could be understood between hiccuping sobs, so Brenda simply held them close as her associate began the lesson.

Both kids remained silent during class. When their mother came to pick them up, Brenda mentioned the morning's upset. Their mom said she would speak to them on the way home and that it wouldn't happen again.

But it did. Week after week during the next few months, Luke became more destructive while Emily tried without success to control her younger brother's explosions. Finally, after talking to her senior pastor about the difficulty she was experiencing, Brenda learned the truth. The family was going through a divorce.

With their father gone from the house and their mother dealing with her own issues, the children were left to deal with their own emotions. Brenda learned that Luke was acting out at school—biting, hitting, kicking, and receiving timeouts. Emily became withdrawn and sullen, crying at the slightest provocation. At home, Brenda asked God to give her the words and attitude to love these two children through their struggle. All week, in surprising ways, God brought Luke and Emily to Brenda's mind; each time she prayed for wisdom and strength.

On Sunday morning, Brenda entered her Sunday school room with renewed hope and the realization that helping these children was why God had called her to teach this year. Luke and Emily's mother dropped them off early that day as if she just needed to get away for an hour. But this week, before things could get out of hand, Brenda took Emily and Luke over to the reading corner. After a silent prayer, she began.

"I know about your daddy moving out," she said gently. "That might make you confused and sad." Both children just stared at her. Brenda began to pray aloud as she looked into those blank faces. "Dear Jesus, we know you love us and are always there to help us. Please be with us now on the reading rug and help our hurting hearts." Brenda paused and bowed her head. She felt Luke and Emily lean against her, their little bodies shaking with tears.

"We don't know how to fix things, Jesus, but we trust that you do, and that you will. We trust that you'll help us go on. We know you love us and that you'll never, ever leave us."

The remainder of the year wasn't easy. There were times when Brenda had to remind herself to love Luke and Emily. But each week as the children came into the classroom, they headed to the reading rug for prayer with Brenda. Little by little, these children began to recognize that with God's help, some of their hurt and anger was healing.

Care and Counseling Tips

THE BASICS

The changes caused by divorce touch every individual in the family. Two-thirds of all kids experiencing divorce show changes in academic or social behaviors. It's helpful to view divorce not as a single problem or event, but instead, to focus on changes caused by divorce (such as living in a single-parent home, losing the noncustodial parent, changes in routines) and how these changes affect family members. Also, divorce is a loss that must be grieved. Because of their inability to fully understand, process, and deal effectively with divorce and its effects, children's reactions to a divorce are highly dependent on their age and stage in life.

+ Preschoolers and lower elementary school children.

This age group usually reacts with feelings of sadness, insecurity, and helplessness. Children may have increased tantrums or cry more easily, or they may show changes in their normal eating or sleeping habits. You might notice these young children reacting fearfully when separated from parents, like when dropped off for Sunday school. Children in this age group may revert to talking "baby talk," thumb-sucking, or bed-wetting, or may complain of physical illnesses such as stomachaches.

+ Upper elementary school children.

Older children are more likely to express feelings of intense anger and rejection. They may have feelings of loneliness, sadness, loss, and fear, or might act like they just don't care. Also be aware that children in this age group may become aggressive, or even hostile, to parents and other adults.

+ Adolescents.

Teens who experience divorce are able to better understand the loss, sadness, anger, and pain than their younger siblings. They may express emotions in aggressive actions or might act out, engaging in delinquent and sexually promiscuous behaviors. Teenagers may also resort to using alcohol and drugs in response to becoming depressed and withdrawn. This depression may manifest itself in suicidal thoughts. If a child at any age expresses suicidal thoughts or plans, refer him or her to a mental health professional immediately.

SCRIPTURE HELP

+ **Job 42:1-3**
+ **Psalm 25**
+ **Psalm 28**
+ **Psalm 31**
+ **Psalm 103**

+ **Proverbs 3:5**
+ **Jeremiah 29:11**
+ **Romans 8:35-39**
+ **Romans 15:7**
+ **2 Corinthians 4:7-8**

Care Tips

+ Encourage children to talk about their feelings.

Feelings that go unexpressed can lead to anxiety, fear, and depression. If children are allowed to express their feelings, then they can be dealt with reasonably and lovingly. Children of all ages need to know that communication lines are open.

+ Provide a "feeling" vocabulary.

Young children haven't learned the words to describe the intense feelings they have. Take advantage of everyday experiences to label feelings. Or make a feeling chart (happy, sad, and angry faces), and ask the child to point out how he or she is feeling that day.

+ Provide a consistently warm and stable environment.

Divorce causes upheaval in families, so keeping routines in place for the child and rules consistent will give the child a sense of security.

+ Teach children how to use affirmations about themselves.

When the child does a good job or perseveres at a task, respond by saying, "What a great job! You must be very proud of yourself." By helping the child feel good about him- or herself now, you're creating a pattern for developing healthy self-esteem.

+ Reassure children that they did not cause the divorce.

Children are in a developmental stage where they think everything revolves around them, so many kids worry that their actions or behaviors caused the upheaval in the family. Continually remind the child that the divorce was not his or her fault.

+ Practice effective listening.

Children have many concerns and feelings about their parents' divorce. Many adults find it difficult to listen to children without suggesting a solution to the problem. Adults who listen with patience and caring attentiveness reassure the child that he or she is being heard.

+ Normalize the child's experience.

Families going through divorce sometimes feel isolated and try to keep their issues private. This can intensify a child's insecurity—it's better to let children know that they are not alone in their pain. Find some books about divorce or other family changes. Introduce the child to other children who have experienced divorce or other losses.

Counseling Tips

As families move on and readjust after a divorce, stay involved by using these suggestions:

+ Provide a network of support.

When under the stress of a divorce, some people feel overwhelmed and withdraw from their communities of support. Occasionally they feel guilty and are embarrassed by the divorce and alienate themselves from others who care. Often they are mentally and physically exhausted and do not have the strength to maintain contact. In these cases, the community must reach out. Cards, phone calls, and visits to the home are all important ways to keep in touch.

+ Help with household adjustments.

As parents re-establish themselves separately, they may find that the new challenges of daily living require additional help. Responsibilities such as managing the household finances, doing yardwork, handling repairs around the house, and preparing meals often naturally fall to one spouse or the other, so learning to handle all of those tasks alone can be overwhelming for a new single parent. Offer to help with the practical tasks like mowing the lawn or cooking dinner, or ask if it would be helpful for you to teach the parent one of those skills.

+ Include single parents in activities.

When a divorce occurs, the adults lose their "couple status" and often their circle of friends as well. When hosting a church function, a personal invitation from a church member or pastoral associate is very welcoming.

+ Offer resources.

Act as an ongoing source of information for psychological services, support groups, counselors, helpful books, and child care. You might also be able to recommend some professionals in your congregation or community who can assist the parents with their legal or financial adjustments.

+ Provide a safe and stable haven for children and adults.

Make sure all of the workers in your ministry are aware of any custody concerns. Create strict pick-up and dismissal policies to ensure the safety of all students in your ministry.

WHEN TO REFER

+ When a family member is overdoing.

Using any outlet as an escape (for example, watching too much TV, spending too much time on the Internet, overeating, sleeping excessively, over-exercising, buying or shopping too much, cleaning excessively, over-committing).

+ When abuse is suspected.

+ When a child seems to be taking on the role of the adult.

Or the parent seems to be acting more and more emotionally dependent on the child(ren).

+ When signs of depression occur.

Signs include helplessness, hopelessness, changes in sleeping or eating behaviors, withdrawing from activities.

Additional Care Tips

While divorce has become more prevalent in our society, it has not become less painful. Separation from loved ones, continuing strife between the parents, moving, loss of identity, and social stigma are but a few of the consequences of divorce. The family of God can minister powerfully to fill the voids left by divorce. The church has God's blessing and command to love and care for those who have suffered divorce just as a family loves and cares for its members.

✛ Prayer.

In many ways, our society is at war against marriage. As Christians, our most powerful tool is to pray for the institutions of marriage and family as God intended them. Suggest that once a month, church workers come together to pray for the victims of divorce.

✛ Don't take sides.

The church is called to model forgiveness and reconciliation. One of the best gifts the church can give a family going through a divorce is encouragement to treat the former spouse, and his or her extended family, with respect and civility.

✛ Model Christ-like habits in relationships.

Those who are struggling with the effects of divorce need to witness other Christian families who work through conflict constructively; deal with their children in honest, direct, and supportive ways; and spend time together. Encourage all families in your ministry to pray together, forgive and honor each other—and to have fun together!

What Not to Say

+ "I know just how you feel."

Many of us may think we know how it feels as many of us have come from similar divorce situations. But each child is different and feels his or her pain in a unique and specific way. To indicate you can read the child's feelings disregards the depth of his or her disappointment, pain, and right to the grieving process.

+ "You'll still get to see them."

That's not the point. Life will never be the same again for this child. It will never be as secure and ordinary as it has been up to this point. For younger children, seeing Daddy every other weekend seems like an eternity between visits. For an older elementary child, it can mean managing two sets of household rules, atmospheres, and schedules.

+ "They are better off apart."

This is not the issue from a child's point of view. Often they feel either responsible or at the very least that they could have affected the outcome in some way. Even with parental disagreements or trouble in the home, it was still the life the child knew. Change will take time, and adapting will be tough. He or she will never see either parent in the same way again.

+ "Your dad was wrong to _____."

Don't say anything that criticizes or demeans either parent. Children of divorce are best served when they are encouraged to love and accept both parents. Adults fare better, too, if they are encouraged to treat the former spouse in a civil and respectful demeanor.

+ "God hates divorce."

When spoken to a parent, this type of statement (or "Scripture forbids divorce") may make the person feel guilty, judged by the church, and condemned by God. Unfortunately, the family may be driven away from the comfort and healing that the church can provide. To a child's ears, this statement may cause confusion and guilt—he or she may worry that God's love for the family is conditional and has been lost because of the divorce.

What to Say

+ "I'm here if you need to talk—or even if you don't."

Knowing someone is available to listen to you vent, rant, or cry is a huge comfort. Knowing someone will just be there to be there is also a security a child needs at this point. Sometimes kids don't know how to express their pain so they act out. They need to know someone will stand by and let them process the pain until they can adapt and handle it. This isn't a free pass to create their own "reign of terror," but it is unconditional acceptance.

+ "Can I pray?"

Take the child to a quiet corner, and pray right there with him or her. Model how the child can pray for God to ease the pain and show him or her how to go on. Tell God how much the situation hurts, and ask him to provide peace and healing in the child's life and in the family.

+ "I care about you, and so does Jesus."

This break in the family unit feels like a death, and kids can react by feeling lost, abandoned, and alone. Parents are drowning in their own pain and are often unable to meet the emotional or spiritual needs of their children. Knowing someone cares and will stick it out with them is a huge relief. Teachers still expect them to perform in the classroom, friends expect them to adapt quickly, and their parents are often emotionally absent. They need the stability of Jesus, and you may have been chosen for such a time as this.

+ "Please take care of yourself."

Parents experiencing a divorce need to maintain their emotional and psychological well-being. Encourage parents to spend time by themselves, to do something special for themselves, and to spend time with caring friends. If a parent has a supportive network, it can protect the child from becoming a surrogate spouse and feeling responsible for the emotional well-being of the parent.

ADDITIONAL RESOURCES

+ Books

The Everything Parent's Guide to Children and Divorce. Carl E. Pickhardt. Cincinnati, OH: F + W Publications, Inc., 2006.

Helping Your Child Survive Divorce. Mary Ann Shaw. Secaucus, NJ: Birch Lane Press, 1997.

When the Vow Breaks: A Survival and Recovery Guide for Christians Facing Divorce. Joseph Warren Kniskern. Nashville: B&H Publishing Group, 1993.

+ Online Resources

www.counseling.org (American Counseling Association)
www.exnet.iastate.edu/Publications/PM1640.pdf (Talking With Your Child's Other Parent)
www.kidshealth.org/kid/feeling/home_family/divorce.html
www.kidsturn.org

CHAPTER SEVEN

Legal Trouble

Understanding How It Affects
Children and Families

with counseling insights from RON WELCH, PSY.D.
& JANNA KINNER, MSW
+ care tips from HEATHER DUNN

Cassidy is a pretty girl with a great smile and expressive eyes. She lives with her grandmother in a second-floor apartment. She's lived with her grandmother for 10 years, since she was 2.

Cassidy's mom isn't in the picture much. It seems like she's always in jail, or has just gotten out. Cassidy couldn't tell you exactly what her mom has done wrong, though she's smart enough to know it's probably drug dealing or something like that.

Her mom shows up every so often, with good intentions of getting a job and paying attention to Cassidy. Four years ago, Mom showed up with a baby, Cassidy's new little brother. Things were going to be different now. They were going to be a family. That lasted for a couple of months, and then her mom disappeared again. Now Cassidy's little brother lives with them, too.

Cassidy didn't realize that her life was different from other kids' until she started elementary school. She learned that in most families, Mom is around all the time. Mom comes to school and helps with parties, or is around on a daily basis. Now that Cassidy's in fifth grade, she hears about the arguments that other girls have with their moms about makeup and clothes. It seems funny that she wishes she could argue with her mom, too.

But Cassidy loves her grandmother and knows her grandmother loves her. She doesn't want to be a burden, so she helps with chores and tries hard at school. She and her grandmother talk a lot, but not too much about Mom. They do pray for her, though. And they spend lots of time at church.

Church is a good place where the teachers are nice. No one really talks about her mom, but Cassidy thinks they know. Teachers ask for Cassidy's help when she comes early and always mention scholarships to her grandmother for the camps in the summer. It feels safe. Cassidy has friends from church and school, but she never invites them over. She doesn't want to answer questions about her mom or feel ashamed.

If Cassidy could have one wish, it would be to have a house with a mom and a dad. (She would never tell her grandmother that because it would hurt her feelings.) Cassidy always hopes that her mom will straighten herself out and come home for good. But last month, she found out she's back in jail again. Cassidy doesn't want to know why. Her heart aches, and now she spends lots of time in her room crying. She lets her grandmother think she's doing homework. The shame is back, and the disappointment is deep.

But she'll get over it, at least on the outside. She knows that she has a constant friend in Jesus. And she knows her grandmother loves her. She and her grandmother pray for her mom. So Cassidy will just keep working hard and doing the best she can.

SCRIPTURE HELP

+ **Psalm 9:7-10**
+ **Psalm 27:4-10**
+ **Jeremiah 31:13**
+ **Nahum 1:7**
+ **Matthew 6:9-13**

+ **Matthew 7:7-11**
+ **Romans 8:31-39**
+ **2 Corinthians 5:7-10**
+ **James 1:2-6**
+ **1 Peter 5:6-11**

Care and Counseling Tips

THE BASICS

When the courts get involved in family functioning, parents become stressed, and children can sense the tension in the home. Any legal issue that touches a family can be heartbreaking to children, but there are several specific areas that especially impact kids:

✦ A family member's incarceration.

When a family is suddenly ripped apart by an arrest or imprisonment, the effect on children can be devastating. Children may deal with a vast array of emotions, including shame from what caused the family member's incarceration, fear for what might happen next, or grief from the loss of someone who was usually around. These same reactions may also be present if a family member is facing legal charges but has not yet been arrested or sentenced.

The visiting room in a jail or prison is not a hospitable environment for children to reunite with their loved ones. The rooms aren't warm and inviting places where children feel safe. Instead, they're cold, cement rooms with chairs packed together. Even the playrooms that some facilities build for children are usually small and stocked with old, worn toys and games.

✦ Custody battle.

Although a divorce is rarely a welcome or positive experience for parents, the adjustment can be especially difficult for children (see Chapter 6). This stress is exacerbated when legal issues of custody and child support become severe conflicts. Parents may lose sight of what is best for their kids as they become more and more entrenched in a legal battle. Children of divorce often feel they must side with one parent, which jeopardizes their relationships with both their mother and father. In extreme cases, one parent may even attempt to kidnap the children.

+ Financial problems.

Families may find themselves impacted by a variety of financial issues, such as bankruptcy, unemployment, or a lawsuit. As a result, parents often experience increased depression, anxiety, anger, physical illness, or thoughts of suicide. As financial stress increases, so does strain on the marriage, resulting in a greater risk of domestic violence. Children aren't immune from this tension. As parents take on second or third jobs to cover the bills, kids may not be able to spend as much time with them as usual. As parents struggle to make ends meet, children might not have even basic necessities such as food, shelter, or utilities. This adjustment to new socioeconomic conditions may impact a child's self-esteem or his or her relationships with friends.

ADDITIONAL RESOURCES

+ Books

Custody Battle: A Workbook for Children. Nancy Martin-Finks. Chattanooga, TN: National Center for Youth Issues, 2005.

Family Ministry: A Comprehensive Guide. Diana R. Garland. Downers Grove, IL: InterVarsity Press, 1999.

The Co-Parenting Survival Guide: Letting Go of Conflict After a Difficult Divorce. Elizabeth Thayer, Ph.D. and Jeffrey Zimmerman, Ph.D. Oakland, CA: New Harbinger Publications, 2001.

Financial Planning Workbook: A Family Budgeting Guide. Larry Burkett. Chicago: Moody Press, 1990.

+ Online Resources

www.family.org (Focus on the Family)
www.familylife.com (Campus Crusade for Christ)
www.pfm.org (Prison Fellowship/Angel Tree)
www.fcnetwork.org (Family and Corrections Network)

Care Tips

There are many things that church leaders can do to help families who are facing legal difficulties. When offering services to a family, however, be aware that parents and kids may feel embarrassed, scared, and vulnerable. It is possible that the family may initially resent offers of help because they may not want to admit there is a problem or that they can't handle all of the responsibilities alone. Be patient, and do not try to force services on the family, but simply offer assistance. Trust God to help the family accept what your ministry team has to offer.

+ Encourage communication within the family.

When children don't receive an explanation about stressful issues, they develop fear about the secrets being kept and what the future may hold. Kids then begin to imagine and fantasize about what is happening, and may worry that things are worse than they actually are. Parents who are overwhelmed and concerned by their legal problems may not notice the child's reactions. Encourage the family to talk about the facts of the situation and help the child separate fantasy from reality. Parents should keep these explanations age-appropriate.

This communication is especially important during a custody battle. Many mental health professionals agree that in almost all cases, it is best for children to have some form of a relationship with both of their parents. It may be necessary for one parent to have supervised contact with the children until he or she can demonstrate the ability to provide a physically, mentally, and emotionally safe environment for children. While it's not advisable to lie to children about a parent's negative actions, encourage mothers and fathers to present the other parent in a positive light whenever possible.

+ Discuss budgeting.

Regardless of the kind of legal issue they're facing, family members will be impacted financially. Divorce or incarceration may result in one parent leaving the home, reducing the amount of money coming in. In a lawsuit or bankruptcy, the family will also have to adjust to a new, limited financial situation.

Help the family prioritize essential budget items—food, mortgage or rent, health costs, and utilities. Then suggest that they eliminate as many nonessential costs as possible. It may be necessary to spend family time doing free activities rather than going to movies or on vacations. This may require an initial change in mindset for the family, but the long-term reward of becoming financially stable is worth it.

+ Let kids contribute.

Children will feel better if they are able to help alleviate some of the family's stress. While it's important for parents to shield children from most of the strain being caused by legal issues, it's OK for kids to contribute to family functioning in age-appropriate ways. For example, young children can help by keeping their rooms and common areas picked up, or feeding pets. Older kids may be able to assemble simple dinners while waiting for a parent to come home from work. Working together as a family will create a sense of unity.

+ Maintain routines and predictability.

Legal troubles often require everyone to make major adjustments. Encourage families to keep as many things the same as possible. Predictable family dinners, bedtime routines, and church attendance allow children to feel some consistency in their lives.

Counseling Tips

✛ Help the child grieve.

In the cases of an incarcerated family member or divorce, children liter-ally experience a loss quite similar to a death in the family. While adults are able to realize that the person will be absent for a while, in the child's world, the family member seems to be gone forever.

You can help bridge the gap created by a family member's absence. Talk to the child's caregiver about the situation. Then together you can help answer the child's questions—how long the parent may be in jail, how long the legal difficulties may last, what joint custody arrangements have been made, or how often he or she can visit the sibling or parent. You may have to remind the child of these details as he or she continues to grieve.

✛ Help the child put emotions into words.

Legal issues can involve scary experiences for kids—going to court, seeing a family member arrested, visiting a parent in jail, or witnessing a nasty inter-action between divorcing parents. Children often have a hard time express-ing their feelings, but you can help a child identify his or her emotions.

Try offering a list of words, pictures, or facial expressions that the child can point to as a means of identifying what he or she feels. You can then help the child match some feeling words to the pictures he or she chose. Another idea is to invite the child to draw a self-portrait that shows his or her emotions. These drawings will often reveal the child's true feelings and can start a discussion about how to cope with big feelings like fear and anger.

✛ Facilitate communication with absent—and present—family members.

Absent family members: Be creative about how children could communi-cate with parents or siblings they can't see often—letters, cards, videos, or visits may all be possible. Once the child has adjusted to the fact that the person can no longer live in the home, a great deal can be done to help re-establish communication. Work with the child to create an art project that he or she can take to a visit with an incarcerated or divorced parent. A child will benefit from making something to leave with the parent, as it helps the child to leave a part of him- or herself with the parent.

Present family members: It's also important to support the child's relationships with people he or she does have contact with. Kids sometimes become fixated on the absent family member—the divorced parent who is living in a different house, or the sibling or relative in jail. They focus so much on their anger or sadness about this that they forget the other parent, grandparents, or siblings who are still there for them. Arrange special times and activities for these family members to spend time with the child.

+ Suggest coping strategies that have worked in the past.

Pay attention to what has helped the child be successful during past stressful situations. For example:

Distraction—thinking about something else other than the thing that is upsetting the child.

Verbalizing emotions—talking about the feelings that are upsetting the child.

Writing or drawing—drawing pictures or writing in a journal to help cope with difficult situations.

Staying busy—engaging in fun play activities that take the child's mind off of what is upsetting him or her.

Talking to others who have gone through something similar—finding out one is not alone and other children or adults have experienced similar things.

One of the most powerful things you can do for a child whose family is in legal trouble is to help the child realize that he or she will make it through the stressful time. By helping the child identify what has helped in coping with past challenges, he or she will gain confidence in using those same skills to respond to current feelings.

Additional Care Tips

Church congregations can be extremely helpful during a legal crisis for a family. Your children's ministry team can offer specific assistance to the family that focuses on providing for their current needs.

+ Parenting needs.

When a parent is absent from the home, the caregiving parent may not be used to completing all of the household duties alone and may appreciate an offer of help. In some cases, the parent may not be able to adjust his or her work schedule to get the children to school or extracurricular activities, so the ministry team can help with these daily needs. In other families, a grandparent or other relative may suddenly find him- or herself thrown into a parenting role. You could offer to transport children to their activities, prepare meals, complete housework or yardwork, or pitch in with any other daily chores.

+ Emotional needs.

Whether the legal issues have led to a parent leaving the home or not, it is likely that the caregiver is less available emotionally and physically than usual. God can use your ministry team to meet the children's emotional needs that are not being fulfilled. The team may find God using them in a variety of ways, such as spending time weekly with the child, attending his or her sports games or concerts, or extending an invitation to church activities.

+ Spiritual needs.

Legal troubles often create spiritual crises in families. Older children may wonder about their own choices and morals in light of the choices their parents have made. Children may also be confused about why God would "allow" this to happen, which brings up existential questions about the meaning of life and may lead some children to question their faith.

With both older and younger children, this provides a unique opportunity to use biblical teaching to address the question "Why do bad things happen to good people?" It may also be helpful to talk with children about viewing a parent who is in trouble as a good person who made some bad choices, instead of as a bad person. The many Bible passages that talk about grace and forgiveness (John 1:16; Romans 3:24; and Galatians 2:21, for example) can be helpful in helping children change their perception of a parent who is incarcerated or who is engaging in a custody battle.

+ Practical needs.

As families walk through legal processes, they will need extra support. They may appreciate being referred to a financial advisor, Christian attorney, family counselor (see the When to Refer box on page 95) or other services available in your church or community. A church leader can also help by offering to accompany the family to stressful court appearances.

WHEN CHILDREN BECOME PART OF THE LEGAL BATTLE

Sometimes a child may have to testify in court, either as a victim of a crime or to attest to disputed family allegations. Children may experience fear and anxiety at the prospect of having to discuss personal or painful subjects in front of strangers.

Parents and supporters of the family can help by following these tips:

• If possible, visit the courtroom before the child testifies. Knowing what to expect will lessen his or her anxiety.

• Explain to the child that if he or she doesn't know the answer to a question, it's OK to say so.

• Schedule the child's testimony for a time he or she will not be hungry or tired. Discuss with an attorney ways to help the child feel comfortable in this strange environment—it may be possible for him or her to hold a special stuffed animal or speak to the judge privately.

• Reinforce to the child that it's important to always tell the truth.

What Not to Say

✛ "I'll bet this is hard for you."

Yes, it is hard, but the child may not want that reminder. Instead of suggesting how a child feels, ask him or her to tell you about it. Listen to the child's concerns and hopes. Be encouraging and sincere. Kids know when someone is speaking from the heart.

✛ "Everything will be all right."

Unfortunately, legal problems often end in ways that are unpredictable and sometimes unwanted. Instead of making false promises, it would be much better to talk with the child about the realistic conclusions that could occur.

✛ "See what happens to people who break the law?"

OK, a church leader could conceivably use this statement as a means to reinforce the need for good behavior. This lesson may best be kept for another day. The child is already anxious and fearful, and this is not the right time to try to instill more fear in the child. Also, this will likely only reinforce a negative perception of the parent. It would be much healthier to talk with the child about grace and forgiveness, reminding him or her how important it is to have faith in God, who is forgiving and understands our mistakes.

What to Say

✛ "God will be with you during this time."

The assurance provided in the Bible is quite clear in this area (John 14:1; 2 Corinthians 1:3-4). Although we do not know how God will answer our prayers, he will be with us during our trials. This message can be reassuring to a child who feels vulnerable and scared.

✦ "It's not your fault."

You can help the child avoid feeling unnecessary guilt by repeatedly assuring him or her that none of what is happening was due to anything he or she did. Children often personalize situations and assume they did something to cause the bad event.

✦ "Would you like to be on the team?"

If you are a coach or your kids participate in a sport or activity, include this child. Be sure it's OK with the child's caregiver, and be prepared to do the chauffeuring. Also offer to help with registration or uniform costs. Don't offer if you're not committed to making it work for the whole season.

✦ "What would you like to do for Mother's Day?"

After experiencing traumatic adjustments caused by legal issues, kids may have a tough time on holidays, especially family ones. They don't have the resources to buy gifts, and they may not know who to give gifts to. Offer to take a child to the store to find inexpensive gifts for his or her caregiver, parent, or siblings for Christmas, Mother's Day, or Father's Day. Or let him or her come to your place to make homemade gifts.

WHEN TO REFER

Not all legal issues will lead to the need for a professional counseling referral. However, as with any traumatic situation, there are circumstances under which referral will be necessary:

+ When there is danger to self.
If the child, or anyone in the family, makes threats to harm him- or herself.

+ When there is danger to others.
If the child or family member threatens to harm someone else.

+ When there is suspected child or elder abuse.
See the When to Refer box in Chapter 1 on page 14.

+ When parents degrade each other.
If a parent involved in a custody battle is "bashing" the other parent in front of the children, encourage the family to use a mediation resource and to participate in individual counseling as an outlet for their anger. Continued exposure to this type of degradation of the other parent can be seen as emotionally abusive to the children.

+ When you don't have enough training to help the family.
Sometimes a family's legal troubles will far outweigh your ability to offer tangible assistance. Rather than giving inaccurate advice or nebulous help, it's better to refer the family to someone more qualified to deal with the specific problem and its aftermath.

CHAPTER EIGHT

Moving

Helping Children Adjust
to a New Environment

with counseling insights from **LINDA SWINDELL, PH.D.**

+ care tips from **SHARON CAREY**

The following interview is with a young woman as she recalls a move her family made when she was a little girl.

Comforting Children in Crisis: *How did you react when you found out your family was planning to move?*

Eryn: I'm sure the anticipated reaction of most kids would be to get upset or angry, but my response was to withdraw. I was terribly sad because I absolutely loved where we lived. My parents directed a children's camp, and for a 7-year-old tomboy, it was pure paradise. I had acres of woods to play in, an enormous swimming pool in the summer, sledding hills in the winter, game fields, horses, rabbits, kittens. If the weather was bad, I could play inside cabins or meeting rooms, dress up in costumes from the prop closet, or put on a puppet show in the chapel. Our home was a constant hub of activity with a steady stream of friends in and out. It was my world within a world, and it never occurred to me that it could ever belong to someone else. Coming to terms with the fact that I had to leave it all behind was very difficult.

CCC: *What was most difficult about the move?*

Eryn: I couldn't handle the fact that someone else would be living in my room. I remember a day not long after we'd moved out when my family happened to drive past our old house. I saw a wadded bundle of gold carpet sticking out of a nearby trash bin. I burst into tears when I recognized it as the carpet from my bedroom. It broke my heart to think of my room being dismantled and occupied by another kid. Shedding tears over an old rug sounds insignificant now, as I talk about it, but at the time the sight of that gold carpet completely rocked my world. I selfishly didn't want to share the room that had always been mine.

CCC: *How did you feel packing up your things?*

Eryn: The busyness of packing was hard on everyone. We had to be out of our house shortly after summer camp ended, and at that point we still didn't have a definite place to go. Had there been something visible on the horizon to feel excited about, I may have been able to turn my attention from the old to the new and been less apprehensive. The uncertainty had to be frightening for my parents on a completely different level. I, of course, couldn't understand the emotional roller coaster everyone was riding. I just knew there were a lot of boxes, newspapers, and grumpy people in a house that used to be filled with fun. It made me hate moving all the more.

CCC: *What other feelings did you have as you anticipated the move?*

Eryn: It took a lot of patience to wait for the details of our move to come together. We lived out of suitcases and boxes for many months. For a kid with a limited perception of time and space, it felt like an eternity. The thing I wanted most was my own room where I could play. At some point during this transitory period, I must have made the personal decision to "move in" permanently. I drew dresser drawers on several boxes and arranged them to look like my previous bedroom. I laugh at myself now, but I kept thinking *if only I could get some gold carpeting.*

CCC: *What was it like after the move?*

Eryn: It took me a while to adjust to new surroundings. I would wake up in the middle of the night and not know where I was. My parents were very understanding. If I woke up scared, they would pray with me. Then we'd count five things in my room that were the same as at our old house. I remember my mom sharing how she often felt nervous when she woke up in a new place until she realized that no matter where she went, God was always with her.

Another thing I recall was the feeling of being suddenly disconnected from the kids I used to play with. After our move, I never heard from any of my teachers and very few of my classmates again. As I think back on it, I believe it would have had a stabilizing effect had I received a note or phone call from former teachers and friends I left behind.

CCC: *How did you feel about attending a new school and church?*

Eryn: On the first day at my new school, I woke up with the same feeling I used to get at the dentist's office. I couldn't put my feelings into words; I just knew that I didn't feel well. At school, I spent the morning in the nurse's station with a stomachache. My mom was finally called to come get me. Everyone thought I had the flu. When the same scenario occurred several days in a row and then similarly when visiting a new Sunday school class, my parents realized that I was reacting to the stress of so many new adjustments.

CCC: *How did your transition to a new church compare with starting at a new school?*

Eryn: I was kind of a shy and sensitive kid, so the thought of having a classroom full of new peers staring at me made me ill. I was very blessed to be welcomed warmly by a wise and perceptive Sunday school teacher. She had planned ahead for newcomers, and her approach went far beyond simply sending out a "Welcome to our Class" postcard in the mail. Together with her kids she had created a welcome pack complete with a photo of each child. On the back of the photos, children in the class had each written a welcome note and filled in some blanks about their favorite foods, hobbies, sports, pets, and so on. I remember that one little girl named Emily had a rabbit. We hit it off right away.

CCC: *How long did it take before your new house felt like home?*

Eryn: Because our initial move was not anticipated nor one my family was excited to make, we spent some difficult months in limbo while my parents explored employment and ministry opportunities. We didn't "settle in" anywhere for almost a year. Once we did, the adjustment came more quickly. Building friendships was a key ingredient. The turning point came when I was able to invite kids from church or school over to my house to play. Having others on my turf where I felt comfortable and secure was a huge step of transition.

CCC: *Do you remember anything fun about moving?*

Eryn: I don't recall where the idea of "Ten-Cent Turns" came from, but one Sunday after church my dad took us on a tour of our new town. At each intersection, we would take turns flipping a coin. If the dime landed on heads, my dad would have to turn right. Tails meant turn left. We had great fun—often going in circles. At one point, we turned a corner and came upon an ice-cream shop. I said, "Hey, we had one of those at our old house." We pulled in, and I ordered a familiar favorite treat. I believe ending up at the Sugar Shack may have been my dad's plan all along.

WHEN TO REFER

Usually the stress of moving subsides fairly quickly. However, a major change is sometimes difficult for a child. Even the most resilient child can have difficulty coping with the changes a move brings.

Watch for:
+ **Withdrawn behavior**
+ **Unreasonable fears**
+ **Outbursts of anger or tears**
+ **Reluctance to leave parents**
+ **Difficulty making new friends**
+ **Decreased appetite**

These behaviors, especially if they continue for a few months or longer after the move, may indicate that the child is not adjusting well. Recommend professional help for the child.

Care and Counseling Tips

THE BASICS

Moving can be an unsettling event in the life of a child. Overall, the single most important factor that determines how well a child copes with a move is the parents' attitude. If Mom and Dad introduce the moving process as an exciting adventure, then children will be much more likely to accept the relocation in a positive manner. Also, it's important to remember that the reason for the move influences how quickly children adjust—for example, a family may react differently if the move is a result of a disappointing job loss rather than if the family excitedly chooses to move closer to extended family members.

Generally speaking, younger children cope with the transition of moving better than older children—however, very young children can be easily confused as they watch strangers packing and unpacking their belongings and as they encounter strange surroundings. The biggest concern for school-age children is usually whether they will make new friends and fit in.

Care Tips

When you find out that a family in your church is moving, you can use the following ideas to ease the transition:

+ Give the child a goodbye token.
Find a soft stuffed animal or little pillow to send with the child. This can be a comforting object to hug as a reminder that God (and your thoughts) will be with the child.

+ Provide closure.
On the child's last day in your class, use a disposable camera to take pictures of the child with classmates. Send the camera with the child. You might also provide a small address book in which students can write contact information and goodbye messages.

+ Research the new area.
Encourage the moving child to share any information he or she has about the new house or city. Talking about upcoming changes will help the child adjust.

+ Send a postcard.
A few weeks after the move, have the class sign and send a postcard to the child who moved. Remember to keep the message positive: "We will always remember you, and we know you will have a great time in your new Sunday school class!"

Counseling Tips

You have a unique opportunity to show God's love and warmth during a trying time in a child's life. Try these ideas to help kids in your ministry adjust to a move:

+ Encourage the child to talk about the moving experience.

Open communication and allowing expression of feelings is important for the child at this time.

+ Listen without giving advice.

Active listening is a key to letting the child know that you care. Make good eye contact, lean toward the child, and give a hug or pat on the back after the discussion. Actions are often more effective in conveying concern and love than trying to fix the problem with reassuring words.

+ Share an experience from your own life.

Almost everyone has experienced some type of move in life. By sharing your own experiences, you can normalize what the child is feeling. This will help the child feel less lonely and isolated.

Additional Care Tips

Moving to a new area is a big change, and finding a new church can be stressful. Children may feel shy or apprehensive at first—but your ministry can be a safe, fun place for newcomers.

+ Adopt the new family.

Ministering to new families can be shared by the entire children's ministry. For example, you might invite children to take turns in writing notes to the new child, spending special time with the child during Sunday school or church-sponsored events, or being a "friend for the day."

+ Identify well-adjusted kids for a newcomer to play with.

You can jump-start the child toward making new friends. This is especially helpful to do the very first time the child attends church or Sunday school. Try choosing different kids each week, so the new child's circle of friends grows.

+ Plan a scavenger hunt.

Being new to an area *can* be fun. Organize a family event designed to explore your town—this allows the family an opportunity to learn about new surroundings in the context of a game.

What Not to Say

+ "After you move, you'll make new friends and forget all about your old ones."

God considers friendships far too valuable to simply cast aside. Friends are irreplaceable. Although most children quickly adapt to new settings, they should be encouraged to maintain their old friendships through letters, phone calls, and e-mail. Teach kids to value both old and new friendships.

+ "Don't be sad."

Like many things in life, moving is an adventure filled with many emotions. Leaving friends and familiar places can be sad, especially for young children. Allow a child the freedom to experience a move however he or she desires.

+ "Moving is no big deal."

This comment minimizes the apprehensions a child may be experiencing. Regardless of the circumstances surrounding it, a move is a huge deal and affects each family member in a different way.

+ "God wouldn't want you to be upset."

Saying this leads the child to believe that feelings of sadness, anger, or loneliness are somehow wrong. It may also convey to the child that God only loves us if we act happy. A child should be allowed to experience and express his or her emotions, positive and negative, with the knowledge that God's love is constant.

What to Say

+ "When you move, God packs his bags and comes along, too."

Reinforce trust in God's unfailing presence. Knowing that God is right beside the child wherever he or she goes can stabilize changing circumstances and build faith.

+ "It's OK to be upset."

This statement is best shared with a hug. Situations surrounding a family's need to relocate can vary greatly, and a move can be quite traumatic for some children. Even in a best-case scenario, there will be changes ahead that may make a child feel insecure, angry, or confused. Help children verbalize their feelings, and encourage them to express their fears and concerns.

+ "I'm glad God brought you here."

Welcome a new student warmly, and thank God aloud for bringing him or her to your classroom. Encourage other kids to be friendly and to share information that will help the newcomer feel at ease. Even the courtesy of wearing name tags for a few weeks can help a new child begin to feel a part of the group.

+ "Tell me about _____."

Inviting a child to share memories of his or her old house, church, and friends communicates your interest in the child and his or her experiences.

ADDITIONAL RESOURCES

+ Books

Moving with Kids: 25 Ways to Ease Your Family's Transition to a New Home. Lori Collins Burgan. Boston: Harvard Common Press, 2007.

The Berenstain Bears' Moving Day. Stan and Jan Berenstain. New York: Random House, 1981.

Let's Move Together. Carol M. Schubeck. Orange, CA: SuitCase Press, 2000.

+ Online Resources

www.rpsrelocation.com/kids_issues.htm
www.vanlines.com/family_guide/useful_tips.asp
www.kidshealth.org/kid/feeling/home_family/moving.html (Kids Health)

SCRIPTURE HELP

+ **Joshua 1:9**
+ **Psalm 32:8**
+ **Psalm 34:4-5**
+ **Psalm 139:1-3**
+ **Proverbs 3:5-6**

+ **Nahum 1:7**
+ **Philippians 4:6-7**
+ **Philippians 4:13**
+ **2 Timothy 1:7**

CHAPTER NINE

Special Needs

Supporting Families and Children in Special Circumstances

with counseling insights from **LINDA SWINDELL, PH.D.**

+ care tips from **JAN KERSHNER**

Tony was a little more than 1 year old when his parents began to suspect that something was wrong.

He didn't seem to be responding as much as he had been. They noticed long stares. After a while he didn't turn his head in response to stimuli. They even dropped a stack of books right next to him. No response. Then he started walking at an angle, rather than upright.

His pediatrician said it was his legs—that they should take him to an orthopedic doctor. "I knew in my heart of hearts that it wasn't his legs," said Kathy, his mom. "The Holy Spirit was telling me that we needed to find answers—soon." So began the rounds of more doctors and more questions. "Finally, another pediatrician down the line said that we definitely needed to check out his symptoms. He affirmed my feelings, what I already knew."

They took Tony to a center for autism. "That visit was the longest 45 minutes of my life," remembers Kathy. At 14 months, Tony received a definitive diagnosis of autism. His parents were told that he would never speak. "That's the day the music died for us."

Kathy said she cried for two days straight. She retreated into herself.

She expended her emotions, got it all out. Then she came out fighting. "This is my child," she thought. "God gave him to me, and God will help me help him." Putting all their faith in God, his parents began a never-ending quest to find ways to halt the downward spiral of symptoms, and to turn little Tony's life around.

The tests—MRIs, EEGs—showed nothing. They began occupational therapy three times a day. It wasn't working. Their research continued.

They discovered something called ABA (Applied Behavioral Analysis) Therapy. A controversial program, this therapy uses rewards to force an autistic child to respond. Tony began talking. It was working—but only to an extent.

"The problem," said Kathy, "is that it became scripted." Patients learned what to say to achieve a desired result. "I wanted a feeling, thinking, emotion-filled child. Not a robot."

God led them to the next step, another doctor, a leading specialist in the treatment of autism. This doctor had developed a new treatment called floor-time therapy. They were desperate to get Tony in to see him.

The problem? His next appointment was two to three years out. "But this was a God-driven plan," said Kathy. "A member of his office staff called and was incredulous. 'You won't believe this,' she said, 'but we just got an opening for next month.' " Kathy had no trouble believing. God was giving them the tools to help Tony.

"God gave us Tony for a special reason. We believe he opened doors to new therapies as a way for us to help others. He uses us as catalysts to help other families with autistic children, and he uses our faith to help others rely on God."

How did Tony's autism affect his two older brothers? "We told Conner, who is two years older, that Tony has a special brain and he needs special tools to help him function." His parents invited Conner into Tony's therapy group as a way to involve him.

"The first years after the diagnosis were so intense, I'm sure Conner felt a little neglected. All we could do was to focus on the quality time we had with each of the kids."

Tony's other brother, Sam, was quite a bit older and had apparently been studying autism at school. When his parents told him that Tony had a problem, he responded, "It's autism, isn't it?" His next response was, "We'll get through it."

For now, the family continues the journey together. "Every day is not roses," says Kathy. "But God's grace and goodness are always there. God makes the moments of joy and success better. Our goal as a family is to give back because we've been so richly blessed. We're eager to share tools and techniques. We want to be a resource for others. We see this as our mission field."

And what about Tony? Today Tony is a healthy, high-functioning child who knows he's autistic. But does that hinder him? Just listen to his mom. "He's creative. He's funny. He has incredible insight. He wants to be a filmmaker." And then look at Tony. He's a 5-year-old reading at a second-grade level. He speaks both English and Spanish. He'll go to regular kindergarten next year. And he loves God.

"Tony is our stop-and-smell-the-roses child."

SCRIPTURE HELP

+ **Psalm 46:10**
+ **Isaiah 40:31**
+ **Isaiah 41:10**
+ **Matthew 11:28**
+ **Matthew 19:26**

+ **Mark 10:14**
+ **Luke 11:9**
+ **John 14:27**
+ **Romans 8:28**
+ **Hebrews 4:16**

Care and Counseling Tips

THE BASICS

Children with special needs comprise a large and very diverse group of children. The broad term "special needs" includes learning disabilities, language impairments, mental retardation, emotional disturbances, physical disorders, impairment with movement, and difficulty with hearing or seeing. While each disability is different, there are often similar characteristics.

+ Learning disabilities.

Children with learning disabilities fall within the normal range of intelligence; in other words, they are not mentally retarded. They do have difficulties in school-related areas, especially reading, writing, or math. Children with learning disabilities do not have a problem controlling their emotions, nor do they have trouble seeing or hearing.

+ Attention-deficit hyperactivity disorder.

Children with ADHD have trouble focusing on any one thing and are easily bored. They show extremely high levels of physical activity, find it hard to suppress their emotions, and don't spend a lot of time thinking before they act.

+ Autism spectrum disorders.

Children who are diagnosed with these disorders have symptoms that range from a severe form, called autistic disorder, to a milder form, called Asperger syndrome. However, all children with autism spectrum disorders demonstrate deficits in three areas:

- *social interaction*
- *verbal and nonverbal communication*
- *repetitive behaviors or interests*

Children with ASD do not follow the typical patterns of child development. Some children show differences at birth. In most cases, however, the problems in communication and social skills become more noticeable as the child lags farther behind other children the same age. Some children start off developing normally, but sometime between the first and third years, the deficit behaviors become apparent. Sometimes the change is very sudden, and other times there is a gradual leveling-off of progress.

+ Mental retardation.

Children who are mentally or intellectually retarded function at an intellectual level that is below average. They have difficulties with learning and daily living skills, such as basic communication, self-care (for example, toilet training), and social skills.

Diagnoses range from mild, which is the most common type, to profound, which occurs rarely. Mildly mentally handicapped children develop social and communication skills during their first five years but begin to have difficulties when they enter school. They usually can attain a level of sixth grade in formal schooling.

Moderately retarded children learn to talk and communicate, but usually have poor social skills. With training, they can learn some skills and take care of their personal needs.

Severely and profoundly mentally retarded children, who make up about 5 percent of the mentally retarded population, have poor muscle coordination and limited communication and self-care skills during early childhood. Profoundly retarded children do not reach such normal physical milestones as walking and talking. Typically, these children require constant supervision.

+ Physical disabilities.

The most common types of physical disabilities are hearing or seeing deficiencies, and disabilities that confine the child to a wheelchair.

Care Tips

✚ Understand that grief is normal.

Families of children who have been recently diagnosed with a disability will likely be grieving the loss of having a "normal" child. As the child grows and develops, each new phase of life will bring new challenges, so the family may experience the grief process many times along the journey of raising their child. Remember that grieving is a normal and healthy response to any family change or difficulty.

✚ Recognize the different stressors for the family.

In the months following the diagnosis, the family will likely be struggling with a number of important issues. There will be *financial* stressors, as the family questions their ability to afford the treatment. The family may worry about how they will be affected *socially*, wondering how other children, friends, and church members will react. Parents may also experience *psychological* stress. For example, there may be feelings of guilt ("Did I cause this?") and isolation ("I have to deal with this by myself—no one is here for me"). Parents may also feel powerlessness, as they want to protect and rescue their children from pain and suffering.

✚ Reach out to the family.

Families of children with special needs may feel isolated and lonely. Support them through phone calls, cards, and visits to their home. Reassure the parents and children that the church community cares about them. Be a constant and reliable ally—parents need to know that the church will support them now as well as in the future.

✚ Commit to open and constant communication.

As the child develops, new and different obstacles will confront the family. Open and ongoing communication with parents will help assure the child's continued progress and reassure the parent that the church community is a strong support to lean on.

+ Believe that all children are important.

Remind the family often, through your words and actions, that all children are valuable and precious. Look for the child's unique qualities, and focus on what he or she adds to the family or your ministry.

ADDITIONAL RESOURCES

+ Books

Building a Joyful Life With Your Child Who Has Special Needs. Nancy J. Whiteman and Linda Roan-Yager. London: Jessica Kingsley Publishers, 2006.

Wonderful Rooms Where Children Can Bloom. Jean R. Feldman and Aldene Fredengburg. Peterborough, NH: Crystal Springs Books, 1997.

Ten Things Every Child With Autism Wishes You Knew. Ellen Notbohm. Arlington, TX: Future Horizons, 2005.

1001 Great Ideas for Teaching and Raising Children With Autism Spectrum Disorders. Veronica Zysk and Ellen Notbohm. Arlington, TX: Future Horizons, 2004.

Helping Children With Autism Learn: Treatment Approaches for Parents and Professionals. Bryna Siegel. New York: Oxford University Press, 2003.

+ Online Resources

www.specialchild.com/index.html
www.supportforfamilies.org/internetguide/index.html
www.childrensdisabilities.info/vision/freebooks.html

Counseling Tips

The church can play an important role in the ongoing care of a family with a child with special needs.

+ Educate yourself.
Learn as much as you can about the child and the specific disability, including finding local experts, resources, and programs.

+ Involve the parents.
In serving children with special needs, it is important to maintain close relationships with parents. Parents know best what their child's capabilities and needs are. This also reassures the parents that they are not alone. Keeping parents in the loop when planning lesson plans, trips, and other activities will allow special needs children to more fully participate.

Be sure to include both parents when possible. When both parents are actively and positively involved in their children's lives, children are more likely to lead healthy, productive lives.

+ Communicate, communicate, communicate.
Regularly sharing information about how the child is doing is important. For example, keep a communication book to note any changes at home, school, or church.

+ Respond to the child, not the disability.
Sometimes, when a child has been labeled, others "see" the label and not the child. This child has a disability, not an inability.

+ Don't lose hope.
Recognize that you can make a difference in this child's life!

Additional Care Tips

+ Don't forget the other siblings.

Every child in the family must adjust to having a brother or sister who is "different." Remember that each child will work through this adjustment in his or her own way.

+ Provide respite for the family.

Caring for a child with special needs on a short-term basis is a wonderful gift that the children's ministry might offer the parents.

+ Make your ministry accommodating.

Meet with the parents of a child with special needs to determine any accommodations your program will need to make. Providing a sign language interpreter, extra help with any written activities, or an adult partner can help the child feel more comfortable and involved.

+ Finding partners in the secular society.

Many organizations are dedicated to serving the special needs population. Examples include Goodwill, Salvation Army, Association for Retarded Citizens (ARC), and Volunteers of America. These organizations, and others, have many programs in place for training and serving children and adults with special needs.

What Not to Say

+ "Are your other children normal?"

Having a child with special needs affects every member of the family, often splintering them apart just when they need each other the most. Make sure your comments are directed to building up the family as a whole, rather than creating more distance with uninformed and hurtful comments.

+ "God won't give you more than you can handle."

While this is true, parents who are overwhelmed with shock and grief may already be feeling that God has given them too much. A statement like this may make parents feel guilty or angry at God.

+ "I'm so sorry for you."

Children with special needs have a lot to offer their families, churches, and communities. Choose encouraging words to help parents find the strengths in their children.

+ "Just listen to the doctors."

Though medical professionals are very helpful in diagnosing and suggesting treatment options, it's also important for families to be informed and involved. Encourage parents to do research, ask questions, read books and check websites for information about the child's diagnosis, and keep medical files. Parents can make a big difference in their child's treatment by being proactive and seeking out new treatment methods.

What to Say

+ "Please know that you're not alone in this."

When faced with rearing a child with special needs, parents often feel isolated. Gently reminding them that the church is there is a good first step in supporting them.

+ "I'll pray for you."

Knowing that others are petitioning God on their behalf, and are asking God to guide them, can be an immense help to a struggling family.

+ "How can I help?"

Help comes in many forms. Maybe it's a dinner after an exhausting day of testing. Maybe it's an offer to take siblings to a special outing. Maybe it's offering to take notes at doctor visits, or compile research. The simplest way to find out how best to help is to ask.

+ "I trust God has a plan."

Affirmation that God is in control can be a real form of support to a special-needs family.

WHEN TO REFER

Usually the child with special needs is under regular care from a team of professionals, including physicians, psychologists, and social workers. As a result, rather than the child with special needs, it is more often the parents or siblings who might require referral services.

+ When a family member is excessively using any outlet as an escape.

Watching too much TV, spending too much time on the Internet, overeating, sleeping excessively, over-exercising, buying or shopping too much, cleaning excessively, over-committing, and so on.

+ When a family member shows signs of depression.

Helplessness, hopelessness, changes in sleeping or eating behaviors, withdrawing from activities.

+ When abuse is suspected. (See Chapter 1.)

CHAPTER TEN

Substance Abuse
Supporting Children Who Deal With Issues in the Home

with counseling insights from
JENNIFER WHITE, LCSW, CACII
+ care tips from **HEATHER DUNN**

As long as I can remember, my mom's been gone more than she's been around. I don't know who my dad is. My mom shows up every so often, maybe once or twice a year. She'll stay with my grandparents and me for a week or maybe a month and then disappear again. She'll be nice to me and give me hugs and say nice things to me. Then I'll get up one morning and she'll be gone.

One summer I asked my grandma where Mom went, and she said Mom was sick and getting help. So that's what I told my friends. I noticed that at my friends' houses, it was the grandparents who came for a visit and the parents who stayed. I asked more questions, and that didn't make my grandparents happy. I learned it's not a good thing to talk about my mom's illness.

My grandparents are cool. They buy me almost everything I want. I have my own TV and my iPod. I have to have noise all the time. I'd go crazy without it.

At school, I collect friends. I laugh real loud and crack lots of jokes. My teachers get after me for talking too much. My friends think I'm bossy, so sometimes we fight. That's OK, I'm used to it. Besides, I like the attention when we're fighting—or making up or whatever. I have a boyfriend, too. Not everyone in fourth grade has a boyfriend. We write notes to each other, and I send my friends to ask him questions all the time.

In school I raise my hand and answer lots of questions. I don't really care if I have the right answers. I'm pretty good at comebacks when I'm wrong. I always volunteer when we're going to act things out or when they need someone to stand up front. I like getting attention.

I get attention at church, too. And lots of hugs, too. My grandma drops me off every Sunday, and my teachers are nice. I go early so I can sing in the choir, and I come back on Wednesday nights for the kid stuff.

I'm not sure about God, though. If he makes church such a nice place, I'm OK with that. I've heard plenty of the stories about him and believe they're true. If the cool adults at church say he's alive, I'm good with that. They talk like he's their best friend. I haven't figured that out yet. I want to believe, I just need more time to make sure he'll be around more often than my mom.

The counselor at school tries to make me talk about my mom. I hate that. I make up excuses so my friends won't know why she called me down. She wants me to tell her how I feel about my mom being gone. What a stupid question. How does she think I feel? It makes my stomach hurt to talk about it.

I really would like to have a normal family—who wouldn't? I love it when my mom comes home. She's nice and says she's sorry for letting me down. She promises to stay straight. She gets a job and sings around the house. Then she's gone again. That's the worst. Nothing hurts as bad as when I find out she's gone again. Why can't she keep her promises? Did I do something that made her want to leave? Was I too loud? Did I crack a joke when I shouldn't have? Did I talk too much? Next time, I won't talk so much.

Care and Counseling Tips

THE BASICS

You can't help a child who lives with a substance abuser unless you're aware of the problem. Kids in your ministry may be giving you signs that things aren't going well at home. While the following problems can result from other causes, when you observe them in a child, it's important to consider that substance abuse, particularly parental substance abuse, may be a factor.

+ Look for warning signs in children that a family member (most notably a parent) is abusing substances:

- Emotional or social withdrawal
- Discontinued or decreased attendance at church services and functions
- Recent and noticeable change in behavior
- Covering up for a family member or minimizing the use
- Fear of the using family member
- Problems at school: academic, social and/or behavioral
- Looking disheveled, unkempt, or just inappropriate
- Arriving at church or functions late (kids may be in charge of taking care of themselves)
- Unexplained bruises or burns (injuries due to lack of supervision, or possible abuse by a substance-abusing family member)
- Fluctuation of performance or participation levels, especially when children begin to worry about going home
- Sophisticated knowledge of drinking or drug-use practices, or becoming uncomfortable when alcohol or drugs are discussed
- Hints by friends, such as "Derek is upset because things aren't good at home"
- Stomachaches, headaches, or other physical ailments with no apparent causes

- Parents who are hard to reach, who miss appointments, or who don't show up for functions or to pick kids up

+ Recognize the effects of parental substance abuse in the family.

Children who live in homes where parental substance abuse is the norm suffer a wide range of negative behavioral effects. Often, caring adults aren't sure what to do, and so do nothing. Or they're afraid to get involved. Or they don't want to make matters worse. If you suspect that a child in your ministry is dealing with substance abuse in the home, you *must* get involved. Consider these facts:

- There's a higher incidence of depression, anxiety, and suicide attempts among children of substance-abusing parents.
- Children of substance-abusing parents are more likely than others to become addicted to alcohol or drugs themselves.
- In homes where a parent is abusing substances, physical and sexual abuse of children is more likely.
- A child may suffer economic consequences if a parent loses a job because of drinking or drug use. The family may lose its home, car, or other possessions.

SCRIPTURE HELP

+ **Psalm 91**
+ **Proverbs 3:5-6**
+ **Matthew 6:25-34**
+ **Luke 11:9-13**
+ **Romans 8:28**
+ **Romans 8:38-39**
+ **2 Corinthians 5:17**
+ **James 1:2-5**

Care Tips

+ Be available.

If you sense that a child wants to talk about a troubling home situation, provide the opportunity. Be available to meet with the child after church, offer to share a soda or go for a walk, or even give the child your phone number. The goal is to let the child know that you're a caring adult who is trustworthy and consistent.

+ Pick up the child for church activities.

A child can feel isolated when living in a home with a substance abuser. Often, he or she can't rely on parents for rides to church or school functions. Help maintain the connection between the child and your church community by offering to drive him or her to and from activities.

+ Encourage the child to be a child.

Kids who live in homes with substance abusers are often so busy trying to make the home functional that they forget that they're just kids. Encourage the child to have fun and, hopefully in the process, feel better about him- or herself. Help the child become involved in church, sports, or clubs. Encourage friendships between the child and other kids in your ministry, and set up relationship-building activities to foster those friendships.

Counseling Tips

✛ Be informed.

Be prepared to talk realistically about substance abuse. The last thing you want to do is offer surface platitudes when the child is already living a nightmare because of substance abuse in the home. Before you speak to a child on the subject, become informed about addiction, treatment, recovery, and relapse.

✛ Make sure the child knows he or she is not to blame.

Explain that addiction is not something that one person can do to another. Even if the child's parent says that the child is making him or her drink or use drugs, assure the child that this is not the truth. Emphasize that the child is in no way responsible for the substance abuse—it's not the result of the child's behavior. Explain that the abuser chooses his or her behavior, and will do so regardless of the child's performance. The abuser will change only when the consequences of substance abuse outweigh the benefits.

✛ Make sure the child knows he or she is not alone.

Let the child know that there are lots of kids out there who are just like him or her—trying to cope with substance abuse in the family. Talk about resources for help, and let the child know that many other kids are already receiving help.

✛ Be aware of the roles kids take on in the family.

As a parent's substance abuse develops, everyone in the family plays a part in preserving the family system. Children unconsciously take on roles that present a good image to outsiders and help the child cope with anxiety. Originally laid out by Sharon Wegscheider-Cruse, four of the better-known roles are:

• *The family hero*—The family hero, usually the oldest child, is the perfectionist. This child believes that if he or she is perfect, the substance abuser will be cured. The hero is usually a high-achieving student involved in many activities. On the outside this child appears to be successful and well-adjusted. However, the family hero feels inadequate, because no matter how "perfect" he or she is, the substance abuser continues to drink or use drugs.

It's tempting to praise these kids for what they do, rather than for who they are. Family heroes need affirmation, not approval. Communicate to these kids that they have nothing to prove—they're already good enough because God made them unique, wonderful people.

• *The scapegoat*—The scapegoat is the child who acts out in troublesome ways, and so accepts the family's blame for its problems. They divert attention from the family's secret problem, and are often blamed for the family's problem.

Scapegoats crave acceptance, but they settle for attention. What they need from you is unconditional acceptance and love. That doesn't mean that you have to condone their negative behavior, but it does mean that you can let them know that you'll love them no matter what.

• *The lost child*—The lost child is quiet and withdrawn. Lost children don't draw attention to themselves because they don't want to burden the family. Because they are so often overlooked, they feel lonely and depressed.

You can help lost children by reaching out to them slowly and carefully. If you go too fast, they'll follow their familiar pattern of giving in to your wishes to keep the peace. But if you build friendships with these kids over time, you can encourage them to come out of their shells and express their feelings.

• *The mascot*—The mascot is most frequently the youngest child, whose job it is to be funny. Mascots use their role to protect themselves and the family from stress and tension. They try to mask the pain of the family's dysfunction. As a result, they feel confused and frightened because they don't know how to communicate honestly.

Help the mascots in your ministry by letting them know that all families face stress and tension, and that healthy families face the stress instead of denying it. Assure the mascot that everything doesn't need to be funny—it's OK to have other emotional responses.

+ Realize and reassure.

Realize the myriad emotions and fears that a child from a family with substance abuse is experiencing. The child is probably worried about the abuser. The child feels scared and alone. The child is ashamed and hesitates to have friends over. The child probably feels guilty and responsible.

Reassure the child that he or she didn't cause the substance abuse, nor can he or she cure it. Encourage the child that it's possible to cope with the situation, look ahead, and find enjoyment in life. Have a list of the resources that your church and community offers ready to give the child.

+ Be ready for a fall.

Beating a drug or alcohol problem isn't easy, and relapse is common. Explain to the child that a relapse doesn't mean the family member will never get well; it's a common part of the healing process. Assure the child that you'll be there for him or her throughout the entire process, even during setbacks.

WHEN TO REFER

+ When a child is in danger.

Children are frequently neglected, abused, or mistreated by a family member who is actively using drugs or alcohol, or by the addict's friends. Even if the child hasn't been physically hurt, he or she may be exposed to dangerous and scary situations. Report the situation to your local Department of Human Services or your police department.

+ When a child becomes depressed, struggles in school, or exhibits other problem behaviors.

Children often feel responsible for their family member's decision to use drugs or alcohol—sometimes this leads to depression or increased anxiety. Refer the child to a mental health professional who is specially trained in the area of substance abuse and its ramifications.

+ When the problem becomes physically dangerous.

If you recognize that a person's substance abuse is threatening his or her health or life, or that of family members, contact the police or a substance-abuse recovery program immediately.

Additional Care Tips

+ Let kids know that Jesus can be their best source of love, strength, and healing.

Because the self-esteem and coping strategies of kids from substance-abuse families are often so damaged, they need to hear over and over that Jesus loves them unconditionally. They need to hear that he'll never leave them or let them down. They need to know that his love is the one thing in life they can always count on.

+ Let kids know that they can surrender their burdens to God.

Kids of substance abusers want desperately to control and fix their family problems. When they can't, they feel like failures. Help them understand that by surrendering their situations to God's loving care, they're exchanging their own inadequate power for his all-sufficient power.

+ Provide social support as a team.

Your ministry team can provide support to a child and his or her family as they cope with substance abuse and recovery. For example, you might offer free child care while the abuser attends AA meetings. Or you might set up a schedule for members of your team to be available to the child or family in the event of a crisis.

What Not to Say

+ "Why doesn't he just quit?"

Addiction is a powerful force that often requires years of treatment and multiple relapses before a person is finally able to quit for good.

+ "It's just not fair."

Yes, and victims of substance abuse will be the first to tell you so. These kids didn't ask for irresponsible parents. Be a friend who stays on the brighter side of life. Instead of focusing on negatives, help the child look for positives. Help the child discover his or her gifts and talents and find positive outlets for his or her feelings.

+ "I shared your situation as a prayer concern."

Unless specifically asked to do so, never share a child's personal story with anyone. However, if you learn of a situation that endangers a child or family member, take steps to intervene immediately. Learn the difference between keeping a confidence and keeping a harmful secret.

What to Say

+ "I'm here for you when you're ready."

Addiction can make people feel isolated. Letting all members of the family—including the addict, the spouse, and the children—know that you're there and willing to be a part of their recovery can be very powerful.

+ "It's not your fault."

Repeat this often. Reassure kids that they're not responsible for their families' problems. They didn't cause the problems, and they can't cure the problems.

+ "How about a game of catch?"

Spend time with the child. Offer your friendship. Use simple activities where conversation can happen naturally to develop a relationship. Make sure the child's caregiver knows that you want to be a part of the child's support system, and that you're not trying to pull the child away from his or her own family.

+ "What do you think about...?"

Be a listener. Ask the child about favorite sports teams, favorite music, and favorite school subjects. Showing interest in the child as an individual will give him or her more confidence apart from family problems.

MAKE AN EMERGENCY PLAN

If a child in your ministry is struggling as a result of drug abuse in the family, use the following checklist to help him or her make a personal emergency plan.

• Make sure the child knows how to call the police, fire department, and doctor. Encourage the child to teach siblings the same information.

• Encourage the child to always keep enough money on hand to make a phone call. Give the child the money yourself if necessary.

• Help the child make a list of safe people to call for help. Include your own name and number, or the contact information for someone else on your ministry team whom the child knows and feels comfortable with.

ADDITIONAL RESOURCES

+ Books

Alcoholics Anonymous, Big Book, Fourth Edition. Alcoholics Anonymous World Services, Inc., 2001. (The big book can also be found online at the AA website listed below.)

Drugs, Society, and Human Behavior. Carl L. Hart, Charles J. Ksir, and Oakley S. Ray. New York: McGraw-Hill Humanities, 2006.

Raising Drug-Free Kids: 100 Tips for Parents. Aletha Solter. Cambridge, MA: Da Capo Press, 2006.

+ Online Resources

www.alcoholics-anonymous.org (Alcoholics Anonymous: includes meeting times and locations)

www.na.org (Narcotics Anonymous: includes meeting times and locations)

www.al-anon.alateen.org (Al-Anon and Alateen: programs designed to provide support to the non-using family members)

www.talkingwithkids.org/drugs.html

+ Phone and Mail Resources

A.A. World Services, Inc., P.O. Box 459, New York, NY 10163, 212-870-3400. For information about Alcoholics Anonymous including meeting times and locations.

CHAPTER ELEVEN

Terminal Illness
Supporting Suffering Children or Their Family Members

with counseling insights from LISA DOWNS, LPC
+ care tips from BECKI MANNI

Katy had been a healthy kid all her life. A tomboy at heart, she loved playing outside with her brothers. Though she was the only girl in the family, she could run faster, jump higher, and throw farther than her brothers. Katy loved playing baseball and played fall and spring ball on her brother's Little League team. Until fifth grade, that is.

It had started in January that year, right after the school year resumed from winter break. Katy complained about a backache. Her parents initially thought she might have hurt her back at the playground. But as the month continued, Katy grew more and more lethargic. She would lay her head down on her desk and sleep through class. She came home each day and crashed on the couch, watching TV until bedtime. Her appetite disappeared, and she lost weight at an alarming rate. In Sunday school she curled up in a ball on the rug and just listened to the lesson.

Soon after Valentine's Day, the doctors diagnosed Katy with a rare form of bone cancer. It had started at the base of her spine and was quickly ravaging her small, athletic frame. As her children's pastor, I visited Katy and her family during her initial hospital stay, and I was shocked at how drawn she looked. My heart sank as her parents explained that Katy would soon be treated with chemotherapy but that the chances of her recovering were dismal at best.

I knew my first responsibility was to support this devastated family. How was I to stand there and comfort them without sounding trite? How could I assure them of God's love and his providence? How could I keep myself from questioning his plans? I asked if I could pray with them. I knew I had no solutions. As I began to pray, I heard Katy's mother, Darlene, quietly sobbing and then heard the door close as Katy's dad left the room. I soon ran out of words as my thoughts swirled in confusion and disbelief. I continued to hold Katy and Darlene's hands as we all sat in silence before our all-knowing, all-powerful God and hoped for a miracle.

That was the first day of a long and difficult six months. Katy was allowed to return home, and she desperately wanted to return to school. Darlene asked me to accompany her on a visit to Katy's class. We gently explained Katy's illness and tried to prepare her classmates for the obvious changes in her little body. I was struck with the love and compassion this class of fifth-graders exhibited as they dealt with their own questions and fears. They wanted to know what had caused it, if they could catch it, and how long it would be before Katy got all better. But they also asked questions about Katy's state of mind and how they could help. We answered as best we could, and shared small ways they could help. Katy's stamina would be reduced, and she would need help, such as carrying her book bag or helping her to the lunchroom. Time and time again, they surprised us with their willingness to help and protect their friend.

My own faith was greatly tested and stretched as I watched Katy and her family deal with the situation. Each week in Sunday school Katy looked smaller and more bent over, but a different sort of transformation was occurring as well. She seemed always to be smiling; she had a special glow about her. She loved singing praise songs, and she always volunteered to lead prayer time. It was as if I watched the Holy Spirit visibly inhabit this dying child's body.

Katy lost her hair from the chemo, and by May she could no longer walk. The disease had destroyed her hips and lower back so she could no longer sit. The children at school, in their desire to help, decided to make her a bed in the classroom. They had learned in science class how to recycle plastic grocery sacks into pillow stuffing. Their teacher bought a bolt of muslin cloth and sewed it into three huge pillows. The students went to each classroom explaining their plan, and the plastic bags began to pour in. Within a week the entire school had participated and provided enough plastic bags to stuff the three large pillows. The children spent days decorating each one with permanent markers and fabric paints. Katy kept one in the classroom, she took one home for the family room, and she brought one to Sunday school.

Katy's dad carried her into the classrooms at school and church and laid her down on her pillow. Most of the time she lay with her eyes closed, but at times she was awake enough for someone to read to her. And she loved surprising everyone with spontaneous answers to a math problem when everyone thought she was asleep. Katy's condition opened countless doors to conversations about the shortness of life, how fragile we are, what happens after death, and the assurance we have in Jesus.

Throughout the summer we continued to pray for a miracle recovery, while Katy continued to assure us that she was ready to see Jesus. She was in great pain, and she reminded us that God would take that away when she got to heaven. She was sure she would run and jump and play again in her Savior's love. She had no doubt that he loved her, and she loved him right back.

Katy left us late in July that year. I sat in her hospital room that night with her parents. We prayed for the peace that passes understanding, for relief of Katy's pain, and for the strength to keep going. We held hands, prayed, cried, and I tried to serve this family in pain as best I could.

Care and Counseling Tips

THE BASICS

A child who is dealing with terminal illness, their own or that of a loved one, has the same need for love, emotional support, and normal activities as any adult. The idea of children dealing with terminal illness is difficult to acknowledge and talk about, but a child should never have to deal with any difficult situation alone—especially terminal illness. Reactions to coping with a terminal diagnosis follow a fairly typical pattern.

+ First thoughts.

A common first reaction is to think, "This is all a bad dream." Next, the child may act as if he or she had never been told of the terminal illness. Denial is a protective emotion when a life event is too overwhelming to deal with all at once.

As the illness progresses, the child may grieve the loss of childhood. He or she may grow too tired or lethargic to play with friends. Medications may make the child too ill to engage in favorite activities, and hospitalizations may rob the child of time with friends and family.

+ How kids react.

The age of the child will determine, in part, how he or she reacts to the news of a terminal illness. Young children (up to age 8) will not need a great deal of detailed information regarding the illness or that of a loved one. Older children (ages 8 to 13) will have more questions and concerns. All children will want to know the name of the illness, the body parts involved, and how the illness will be treated.

Children are often unable to express themselves through words. Many express their emotions through their behaviors. It's not unusual for normally well-behaved children to act out or for outgoing children to get quiet.

+ Dealing with fear.

Children will have many natural fears as they face terminal illness. They'll worry what will happen to their family once they're gone, or what will happen to them after a loved one dies.

They may also have fears about physical pain as the illness progresses. Children seek a beginning, middle, and end to a story. Often children will be afraid and believe the worst if they are not given complete information. Children want to know "What is going to happen to me?" or "What is going to happen to the person I love?" If they sense they are not being told the truth, they will fill in the gaps on their own. Give the child information in a simple and direct manner. When answering questions posed by the child, be sure you understand what is being asked, and provide only the information he or she needs at the time. Let him or her know that all feelings are OK to have and to show.

SCRIPTURE HELP

+ Psalm 23
+ Psalm 91
+ Psalm 116:15
+ Isaiah 12:2

+ Isaiah 26:3-4
+ John 14:2-3
+ Revelation 21:4

Care Tips

The diagnosis of a terminal illness creates immense feelings of powerlessness and lack of control. There are a number of positive ways to help and support the terminally ill child or the child concerned about a loved one who is terminally ill.

+ Communicate.

Use language the child can understand, and avoid giving information not requested. Kids often prefer to communicate by nonverbal means. Encourage children to draw pictures of how they feel, of times spent with someone they love who may be dying, or anything they want to express about their illness or that of a loved one.

+ Listen.

One of the most helpful and healing things you can do for a child is to listen to his or her story without judging or offering advice. Avoid telling a child that you know how he or she feels. Never underestimate the importance of a nonjudgmental and caring presence. Use open-ended questions such as "What has it been like for you?" or "What would help most?" Provide a safe place for the child to share concerns, feelings, and fears.

+ Address spiritual needs.

When talking to children about death, share what the Bible says about heaven and the hope we have as believers in Jesus. Reassure the child that Jesus loves him or her. Explain that when we believe in Jesus, we are never alone because he is always with us, no matter how difficult the situation. And when we believe in Jesus, our sins are wiped away and we can live forever with him in heaven. Explain that the Bible says that in heaven there will be no more sickness and no more tears.

Counseling Tips

Trying to cope with a terminal illness or that of a loved one is challenging. When you have to say goodbye to a child or help a child say goodbye to a loved one, the process can be overwhelming.

Don't push the child to talk about his or her feelings. Children need time to grieve and be upset. There's no magic formula for helping a child deal with terminal illness—however, recognizing the following factors may give you insight.

+ The child may worry that he or she did something to cause the illness.

Most children believe that they are to blame when bad things happen. Kids usually don't talk openly about these feelings, so reassure the child even if he or she doesn't bring it up. Emphasize that the illness is not something the child caused. Providing simple, direct explanations regarding terminal illness will ease the child's mind and reduce feelings of guilt.

+ The child may regress.

A terminal illness in the family, either the child's illness or that of a loved one, creates a variety of emotions. Children may begin to act younger by going back to crawling, demanding attention, and talking "baby talk." Regressive behavior is the child's way of telling you that he or she needs to be nurtured. Children may also reveal their feelings through their play—dolls may take trips to the hospital, throw up, and get frequent shots. They may act out through play what they believe their death or that of a loved one will look like. This type of play is a healthy way for them to express their anxiety, fear, and sadness. Sit with the child while the child plays without interjecting what you think should or should not be expressed.

+ Even a dying child needs time to be a child.

If the child is physically able to do so, take him or her to a park, color together, blow bubbles, fly a kite, or read a favorite book. Older children may prefer to spend time with friends, listen to music, or take a drive. Plan fun activities that will allow the child to let loose, laugh, play, and just be a child.

WHEN TO REFER

Deciding if a child needs professional help is best left to the doctors in the case. Your role is to partner with the medical team, since they know best how a child is liable to react at any given stage of an illness.

Discuss with the doctors any of the following changes:

- Lack of motivation or interest in activities that used to be pleasurable
- Inability to sleep, frequent nightmares, decreased appetite, or prolonged fear of being alone
- Imitating the deceased person or making statements about wanting to join the deceased
- Acting much younger than the child's actual age for an extended period of time
- Becoming physically aggressive or expressing thoughts of wanting to harm him- or herself

Additional Care Tips

When a child or family member is facing terminal illness, almost all of the family's energy is directed to the sick family member. Siblings of the terminally ill child may become jealous or feel alone. Parents will become emotionally and physically exhausted. If a family in your ministry is facing a terminal illness crisis, reach out in the following ways:

+ Schedule times for church members to assist with daily activities.
Many families find asking for help difficult. Create a schedule for members of your congregation to volunteer their time to focus on the terminally ill child and family members. Offer to bring meals, pick up siblings from school, or provide respite time for parents. Ask the family to make a list of tasks they would like assistance with, and create a schedule for church families to help out.

+ Have a church ice-cream social or get-together.
Children who are terminally ill need time to play in the same ways they did before the diagnosis. Organize a fun day where the child can play games, throw water balloons, sing, or play catch. Consider the child's safety and medical needs.

+ Prepare a care package.
Create a care package for the child that includes items that help to express feelings and reduce anxiety. Include items such as art materials, modeling dough, favorite CDs, magazines, a journal to write private thoughts in, or a gift card for movie rentals.

+ Offer to pray.
Families of terminally ill children need help in maintaining a sense of hope. Offer to pray for them and with them. Let them know they're not alone.

+ Create a legacy.

A dying child most often wants reassurance that they will not die alone and that they will be missed. Reassure the child that God is always present. Ask the quilters or scrapbookers in your congregation to create a memory quilt or book for the family so the child can see it and even participate in planning and creating the project.

+ Help with finances.

A family facing the terminal illness of one of its members is facing a financial drain. Insurance co-pays (or no insurance at all), trips to the hospital, meals out, lodging, missed work—all take a toll on family finances. But it may be difficult for the family to ask for help.

Address the subject directly, and offer assistance. Take up a collection at church, or have a fundraiser such as a garage sale or auction. Many people will want to help once they know there's a need.

SUPPORTING PARENTS

Parents who are facing the loss of a child due to terminal illness ask themselves over and over why this is happening to their child and what they did wrong to cause their child to become ill. It is important to offer support and encouragement as they face this extremely difficult situation. Reassure them they did nothing wrong and that the illness is not something they could have protected their child against. Remind them of the things they have done to nurture their child, and remind them of ways they can continue to do so. They can continue to rock their child, sing to him or her, massage the child's skin, or watch a favorite movie with the child. Remind them to care for themselves by eating right, taking time away, and asking for help when they need it.

What Not to Say

+ "Time heals all wounds."
Time may dull the pain, but the pain of losing a child is beyond comprehension. This trite expression will ring hollow to someone facing such an enormous loss.

+ "God never gives you more than you can handle."
While true, this statement isn't the best thing to say to a family already feeling overwhelmed and stressed by the diagnosis. Some may be angry at God or wonder why he would bring something so difficult into their lives. Making this statement may increase anger and resentment.

+ "Death is painless."
Sometimes death is not quick or painless, and telling a child he or she will not experience pain is inaccurate. It's best to leave this conversation to doctors or other professionals involved in the care of the terminally ill.

What to Say

+ "I remember all the fun things we have done together."
It's perfectly acceptable to talk about fun you experienced with the child and family members. Reviewing fond memories reminds children and families of good times shared together.

+ "I'm thinking of you and your family."
Terminal illness can make children and their families feel isolated and alone. Letting them know that you're thinking about them, caring about them, and praying for them will comfort them.

+ "May I pray with you?"

Prayer connects us to God, and that's where a fearful or grieving family needs to be. God is the only one who can truly calm our fears or heal our broken hearts. Offer to pray with the family, or say the words for them if they're unable.

+ "I'm here for you."

Most people in this amount of pain cannot express themselves at first. Knowing you're there to hold a hand, to sit quietly with them, or to listen when they're ready to talk is one of the greatest gifts you can give. Prepare to be there over the long haul. Recovery can take time, and they will need you down the road, too.

+ "What do you need?"

At a time like this, everyday life can be overwhelming. Meals are often the first things people offer, but there needs to be a plan for their delivery (no one can eat 40 casseroles in one week). In addition to bringing meals, offer to baby-sit the other children, mow the lawn, clean the house, or do the laundry. Helping with mundane tasks can be a huge gift.

ADDITIONAL RESOURCES

+ Books

When Dinosaurs Die: A Guide to Understanding Death. Laurie Krasny Brown. Boston: Little, Brown, and Company, 1996.

What About Me? When Brothers and Sisters Get Sick. Allan Peterkin, M.D. Washington, D.C.: American Psychological Association, 1992.

How It Feels When a Parent Dies. Jill Krementz. New York: Knopf, 1988.

The Saddest Time. Norma Simon. Morton Grove, IL: Albert Whitman and Company, 1986.

CHAPTER TWELVE

Tragic Personal Loss
Supporting Children and Families Struck by Tragedy

with counseling insights from SHAUNA SKILLERN, LMFT
+ care tips from LARRY SHALLENBERGER

In 2001, a fire burned nearly a third of the building housing Grace Church. The fire was started by an arsonist, which further heightened the trauma to the congregation.

In fact, the entire community experienced feelings of violation and loss. The church was a comforting and familiar sight, having been at its current location for more than 50 years. The section of the building most affected by the fire was the center of many memories of congregational life.

After the fire, however, the primary need wasn't to protect the fond memories of the older generation, but to temper the impressions that the fire had made on the youngest members of Grace. In recent decades the damaged area had functioned as the children's wing. Parents and church members were afraid that the children's sense of security would be disrupted when they saw pictures of their burning children's wing in the newspapers and on the evening news.

A handful of leaders of the children's ministry team assembled to develop a plan to help the children adjust emotionally to the loss of their space.

First, the team realized that children take their emotional cues from the adults around them. So Grace Church held a special session for

Sunday school teachers where they could process their emotions about the fire together. Then they shifted their attention to helping Grace's children process their loss.

The team focused on establishing a sense of security for the children in their ministry to keep them from constantly worrying "What's next?" The team immediately converted the adult education space into a temporary children's wing. They either suspended adult classes or held them across the street at a local retirement home. They replaced destroyed curriculum and hastily purchased new classroom supplies. They erected a new stage, similar to the one that was destroyed, and replaced the PA system. Within a week, children's church was back in business.

But the team neglected one very important task. No one actually talked to the kids about what had happened. In fact, teachers and parents had been trying to skirt around the issue.

They decided to make a matter-of-fact announcement, giving just the information that would be helpful and calming. After the announcement, they allowed a time for questions. Realizing that children process negative emotions in small pieces over time, the team knew that their work wasn't done. They had laid the groundwork for healing, but it would take time before the kids—and adults—in the church would be able to completely move on from this tragedy.

Care and Counseling Tips

THE BASICS

A tragic personal loss such as a natural disaster, car accident, or fire is a scary, sudden, and sometimes even violent experience for a child. The trauma a child experiences during these events can leave long-lasting emotional wounds. Supporting children and their families after a traumatic event can lessen the dramatic impact the event might otherwise have on their lives. In order to help, it's important to know what emotions the child will go through. There are several stages of emotions to consider.

+ First: shock and confusion.

Shortly after a traumatic event, a child's mind will not be able to work as it usually does. The child may appear stunned and respond to things you say without much thought. You'll see physical symptoms of stress such as shaking hands or sweating, but the child will probably have little emotional response at this stage.

+ Second: emotional response.

After the initial shock has passed, a child will start to feel the emotional effects of the event. You may see:

• *Increased anxiety*—sensitivity, asking a lot of questions, talking about things he or she is afraid of, worrying the tragedy will happen again, fear of sleeping, nightmares.

• *Clinginess*—fear of separation from parents or caregivers, asking where his or her parents are, difficulty going to school or church.

• *Anger and resentment*—lashing out at loved ones, expressing anger at the tragic event.

• *Regression*—reverting back to younger behaviors such as whining, crying, clinging, or bed-wetting.

+ Third: returning to normal life.

After a few weeks, the child will begin to adjust back to his or her routine. The sooner the schedule can be re-established, the quicker the recovery. At this phase, the child may start to go through a grieving period for what he or she has lost, but will be better able to manage emotions at this point.

Children experience trauma in different ways at different ages. Here's an overview:

• *Birth to 6 years old:* Infants won't be able to describe what happened to them, but they will be aware of it. They may be more irritable, want to be held more, and cry more frequently. Toddlers and preschoolers will likely express a lot of fear when separated from their parents.

• *7 to 10 years old:* At this age, children start to fully understand that loss is forever. They could become obsessed with thoughts of what happened and have trouble focusing in school. It is likely that they will want to talk about the tragedy often. They may express intense emotions of sadness, anger, and fear that it could happen again.

• *11 to 12 years old:* The reactions of a preteen are similar to those an adult experiences, but kids this age may not have the ability to express their intense emotions as well as they'd like. This could lead to reckless behaviors—to try to avoid those feelings—or to being so consumed by fear that they're afraid to participate in activities they once enjoyed.

Care Tips

+ Go to the child.

Children need a lot of support and reassurance after a traumatic event. Knowing that there are people who are willing to help will comfort kids and help them feel safe. It's important to go to the child instead of offering to take care of the child somewhere else. Immediately following a tragedy, children feel safest when they are close to their parents or trusted caregivers, in familiar surroundings if possible.

+ Comfort the parents.

Most of the child's emotional support is going to come from the parents. Children whose parents deal well with a major stressor will recover more quickly and feel more secure. Help parents formulate a way to talk about the event calmly and matter-of-factly. Offer enough information to help the child understand what happened, but don't dwell on the subject or offer details that might frighten the child further.

+ Offer basic needs.

If a family has lost their home or many of their belongings, they are going to need special assistance. Work quickly with church members, other churches, and local agencies to accommodate the basic needs of the family.

+ Listen.

Let the child tell his or her story. Talking about what happened helps children organize their feelings and process emotions. Don't judge or give advice—just listen. Because each child's timetable for recovery is different, follow the child's lead. Encourage the child to share pieces of the story as he or she is ready.

+ Pray.

Praying with the child will demonstrate not only that you care, but that

God cares, too. It's possible that the child might feel too overwhelmed, or even too angry, to pray. But knowing that someone is interceding for him or her at a spiritual level will touch the child at some point in the healing process.

SCRIPTURE HELP

+ **Lamentations 3:22-23**
+ **Habakkuk 3:17-19**
+ **Matthew 6:25-34**
+ **John 14:27**
+ **John 16:33**

+ **Romans 5:3-5**
+ **Romans 8:18**
+ **Romans 8:35-39**
+ **2 Corinthians 1:3-4**
+ **Philippians 4:4-7**

Counseling Tips

+ Share important information.
The child is going to wonder what happened and why. The more he or she knows, the less scared the child will be. Answer questions honestly, and tell the child what you know. But be sensitive and share only age-appropriate details. If you don't know an answer, it's OK to say so.

+ Let the child see your feelings.
Children don't understand what to do and how to react, and look at the adults in their lives to give them clues. Be honest with the child about your feelings, and encourage parents to do the same. While you want to shield the child from any hysterics, it's healthy to show him or her that sharing emotions is OK.

+ Give information about the future.
The child will likely have many fears about whether such an event will happen again. Talk to the child about what is being done to protect him or her should a similar circumstance take place. For instance, work together to develop a fire-escape route at their new home if their previous house was destroyed by fire.

+ Keep listening.
Being able to discuss feelings will help the child process what happened and recover faster after the trauma. It may take time to move beyond the shock and fully discuss what happened. A child will probably want to keep telling the story as feelings about the event change.

+ Allow the child to help.
Adults and children feel helpless after a disaster or loss. Coach the parents how to give the child small tasks such as taking care of pets,

distributing water to those who have come to help, or picking up trash from safe areas of the yard.

+ Return to a normal schedule as soon as possible.

Encourage the family to return to a normal routine as quickly as possible. Although this will be difficult because the child may be scared to leave the parents early on, return to the routines that include mealtimes, bedtime, playtime, and church. The predictability of a daily routine will help the child feel safe.

+ Encourage recreational time.

As the family tries to get their life back in order, the child will need some fun time away from all the chaos. Encourage the family to engage in simple, fun activities they used to enjoy. Doing so will give everyone a much-needed break.

WHEN TO REFER

It's normal for a child to have increased fears, separation anxiety, clinginess, regression, nightmares, and intense emotions shortly after experiencing a traumatic event. However, some children may develop more severe reactions. If a child has flashbacks, night terrors, nightly bed-wetting, or the inability to return to a normal routine after two weeks, then professional assistance from a trauma counselor may be in order.

Additional Care Tips

After a traumatic event, those affected tend to operate in a state of chaos and bewilderment for a time. Children, especially, need a lot of extra support because they can't process what happened in as full or philosophic way as adults. The continued assistance of people from church can be a huge blessing.

+ Work together on rebuilding.

Include children in practical ways to help them recover from a traumatic event. For example, if your church burned and your children's ministry supplies were destroyed, let kids help make the list of replacements to buy. If your community suffered a natural disaster, encourage kids in your church to help minister to those affected. They could help deliver food to a local shelter or collect toys for children whose homes were lost.

+ Help replace belongings.

Make a list of the things the family needs, and organize donations from your church. People often want to give generously during times of need, but, while laudable, too many donations could overwhelm the family. Appoint a person to be in charge of each ministry area, such as meals, transportation, and spiritual care.

+ Create a group card.

Encourage kids in your ministry to create and sign a group card or picture for the child or children affected by the traumatic event. Due to the many demands after a trauma, the child may not be able to attend church regularly. But think how gratifying it would be for the child to know that he or she is thought of and missed! Plus, the children in your ministry will feel good about reaching out to someone they care about.

+ Offer play dates.

There may be times that the child just wants to play with friends and forget about what's going on. Talk with parents of other children at church about arranging play dates. This may have to be done after the initial shock of the ordeal is over so the child feels comfortable leaving his or her family.

+ Pray.

Last, but never least, pray. Pray for the child yourself, and set aside times for the kids in your ministry to pray, too. Encourage the children to pray on their own as well.

ADDITIONAL RESOURCES

+ Books

How to Talk to Your Kids About Really Important Things. Charles E. Schaefer and Theresa F. DiGeronimo. San Francisco: Jossey-Bass Publishers, 1994.

A Terrible Thing Happened: A Story for Children Who Have Witnessed Violence or Trauma. Margaret M. Holmes and Sasha J. Mudlaff. Washington, D.C.: Magination Press, 2000.

What Happened to MY World? Helping Children Cope With Natural Disaster and Catastrophe. Jim Greenman. Watertown, MA: Comfort for Kids, 2005.

+ Online Resources

www.redcross.org
www.fema.gov/kids (Federal Emergency Management Agency)
www.connectforkids.org/node/392

What Not to Say

+ "You should be grateful. There are children who have it worse than you."

This might be true. However, it sends the message to the child that he or she never has the right to complain or feel loss. If a child buys into this line of thinking, he or she will learn to repress instead of express feelings.

+ "This can't happen again."

We'd like to believe that the disaster or traumatic loss is an isolated event in a child's life. Avoid making false reassurances that may not be true. Instead redirect kids to see God as their forever friend who will never leave them and who will be there during every trial.

+ "It will all be better tomorrow."

You want to reassure the child, but you don't want to give false hope. It will take a while for things to get back to normal and for the child to start feeling better—it's better to be upfront about that.

+ "Be brave."

It's natural for a child to have fears after a tragic personal loss. Telling the child to be brave can give the impression that those fears are not OK to have.

+ "You poor thing, how will you ever get over this?"

While you want to support the child's feelings, you don't want to feed into feelings of helplessness. You want to give the child hope that things will get better, even though they may be hard right now.

What to Say

✚ "I'm right here."
Reassure the child that you want to help and intend to do so for the long haul. Your physical presence after a personal tragedy will be just as important as your words. Let the child know that you are there to help with whatever he or she needs.

✚ "I'm so upset about what happened to your house, but I'm so glad everyone is safe."
Acknowledge the traumatic event and don't minimize it, but also try to offer some positive thoughts.

✚ "It's no one's fault."
Children may not fully understand why an event happened, and as a result, they may feel guilty that they did something wrong. Reassure the child that tornados, hurricanes, and other natural disasters, as well as accidents and illnesses, are forces that the child had nothing to do with and couldn't have prevented.

✚ "Would you help me make an emergency plan?"
You can calm a child's anxieties by helping him or her contribute to a plan to cope with the event if it were to happen again. If a child experienced a fire, allow that child to draw an evacuation map and to test the fire alarms.

✚ "Do you need extra time with me?"
After a traumatic event, sometimes a child just needs to spend time with a trusted adult. The child might not need to discuss anything. But just playing a board game with a loved adult can replenish a child's sense of security and well-being.

YOU WANT TO HELP,
BUT YOU DON'T KNOW HOW...

Everyday your friends and family are confronted by life's challenges...divorce, depression, unemployment, cancer, and more. You want to comfort them but where do you start? What do you say? What if you make them feel worse?

These easy-to-understand guides will give you the confidence to share God's love and comfort with hurting children, teens and adults.

Each book contains twelve topics with:

Sample case studies
Counseling and care tips,
Practical advice,
Scripture connections,
additional resources, and more.

You'll understand what your friends are feeling, what to say, and even what not to say as you help them cope.

Comforting Children in Crisis
ISBN: 978-0-7644-3829-5

Comforting Teens in Crisis
ISBN: 978-0-7644-3830-1

Comforting Friends in Crisis
ISBN: 978-0-7644-3832-5

Comforting Women in Crisis
ISBN: 978-0-7644-3831-8